THE FRAMEWORK OF NĀGĀRJUNA'S PHILOSOPHY

BIBLIOTHECA INDO-BUDDHICA NO. 35

The Framework of Nāgārjuna's Philosophy

A. M. PADHYE

SRI SATGURU PUBLICATIONS
A Division of
INDIAN BOOKS CENTRE
INDIA

Published by
SRI SATGURU PUBLICATIONS
Indological and Oriental Publishers
a Division of :
INDIAN BOOKS CENTRE
40/5, Shakti Nagar,
Delhi-110 007
INDIA

First Edition—1988
I.S.B.N.—81-7030-124-6

Printed in India at :
Kiran Mudran Kendra
A 38/2 Maya Puri **Phase I**
New Delhi-110064

TABLE OF CONTENTS

CHAPTER III

ŚŪNYATĀ 54-92

CHAPTER IV

NIRVĀṆA 93-125

CHAPTER V

ABBREVIATIONS

ERE   =   Encyclopaedia of Religion and Ethics

IPQ   =   Indian Philosophical Quarterly.

JIP   =   Journal of Indian Philosophy.

ACKNOWLEDGEMENT

The present publication The Frame-work of Nāgārjuna's Philosophy' is a reproduction of my research work for my doctoral degree carried out under the supervision of Dr. M.P. Marathe. Discussions with him on general topics of philosophical interest stimulated me to choose the problem for research from Indian classical philosophy. Discussions with him on the subject and his valuable guidance helped me a lot in my work. I really owe much to him. It is not a matter of exaggeration in saying that his help in every respect alone could make me reach the desired destination. I am very much indebted to him. I suppose, it is my duty to express my gratitude to the authorities of Poona University Pune, for allowing me to publish this Ph.D. work.

I am also grateful to Dr. Barlingay and Dr. Sunder Rajan, Head, Department of Philosophy, Poona University, for their guidance and making the departmental facilities available to me. I am also thankful to other teachers from the Department for their valuable cooperation.

I am indeed grateful to the University Grants Commission for awarding me the 'teacher fellowship' under the Faculty Improvement Programme and the authorities of the Sonopant Dandekar College, Palghar, Dist. Thane for deputing me as a Teacher Fellow for three years.

It will be indeed unjust if I do not mention the names of Dr. L. B. Mantri and Dr. Pradeep Gokhale and pay my thanks to them. The former being Head of the Dept. in my parent college, encouraged me on every count to undertake and complete this research work while latter helped me in reading the original Sanskrit texts—Madhyamakaśāstra and Vigrahavyāvartani. I am really grateful to both of them.

Similarly, I am also grateful to the authorities of Jaykar Library, Pune, Deccan College Library, Pune, Bhandarkar

Oriental Research Institute, Pune, S. P. College Library, Pune and the Library of Sonopant Dandekar College, Palghar.

My sincere thanks are due to my colleague, Prof. P. D. Sirdeshmukh and Prof. V. M. Puranik, who helped me in proof correction, compilation of Index and other related work. I am equally grateful to the Proprietor and workers of Kiran Mudran Kendra, New Delhi for their sustained efforts for getting this work printed as early as possible.

My thanks are also due to Shri Naresh Gupta, Director, Indian Book Centre, Delhi and the Proprietor of Sri Sat Guru Publication for undertaking this work for showing light of publication. I am really thankful to them.

I am equally grateful to my family members, my friends, colleagues and wellwishers without whose support it would have been impossible for me to undertake and complete the work. I may, therefore, be allowed to record my sincere thanks to all of them.

31st, November 1987

A. M. PADHYE

(x)

INTRODUCTION

Background of the Present Study

Classical philosophical thought—Buddhist or non-Buddhists, oriental or accidental, ancient, medieval or modern—has been attracting attention of scholars time and again, and the tendency in this direction is being manifested repeatedly. In fact, it is in this kind of attraction being felt about classical thought that its continued significance and importance lies. Such an attraction about classical thought may be felt principally for two reasons : (1) On the one hand one's aim may be to understand and comprehend not only the classical thought alongwith its prominent implications—philosophical, methodological or otherwise—but also to study and articulate the conceptual framework that may be in its background. (2) On the other hand, one's aim may be to study contemporary relevance and significance, if any, of the classical thought under consideration. These two aims may not be necessarily be sought to be accomplished in isolation from each other. They might be sought to be accomplished together. But two things in this connection should be borne in mind carefully : a) The second aim cannot be significantly accomplished unless considerable amount of clarity in comprehension and understanding emerges on the count of the first aim. Despite this, it is often noticed that scholars venture to accomplish the second aim without requisite clarity on the side of the accomplishment of the first aim. As a result, such efforts turn out often to be both abortive and non-illuminating. Something of this kind happens to be the case not out of an accident. It is often forgotten—also not properly understood—that it is in vain to try to accomplish the second aim without accomplishing the first. Otherwise, one might try to study relevance of certain classical thought without bothering to comprehend what precisely that thought is, of which one is studying such relevance. b) The first aim alone may be expected to be accomplished in isolation from the second. This may be done for the sake of the convenience of keeping the study that is undertaken within a manageable limit. On the contrary, the contemporary significance of a given classical thought may not be traced for the very simple reason that it has not been discovered at all or perhaps because it is troublesome to state it in the contemporary intellectual atmosphere. What is important, however, to understand is that, the first of the two above-mentioned aims may be sought to be accomplished in isolation from the other, and in doing so, the sort of study under consideration may not involve a serious kind of shortcoming. It cannot nonetheless, be said that a given classical thought has no contemporary significance and relevance at all. For, subscription to this view brings in a very serious kind of lacuna in the classical thought under consideration in so far as a classical thought that lacks any contemporary significance whatever does not remain classically so important, whatever other significance it may have. This being the case, a study of the contemporary significance of a classical thought of a certain kind cannot be avoided on the ground that it has none.

The present study hopes to accomplish the first of the two above mentioned aims with reference to Nāgārjuna's philosophy. It may, however, be asked : in so far as many scholars—both Indian and western—have already undertaken to study and articulate the philosophy of Nāgārjuna. understanding its classical relevance and significance, where is the need for one more study of the kind that we propose to undertake? Given that number of articles are written on Nāgārjuna's philosophy, that it is presented in its historical setting and also given that some of its tenets have been comparatively tried to be understood, is not the sort of study that we want to undertake unnecessary and therefore dispensable? Just on the ground, the objection continues, that Nāgārjuna's philosophical thought is classically important one need not be the basis of proliferating intellectual world with its studies which bring in and state the same significance of it. For, such an exercise may turn out to be, other things remaining the same, a non-content increasing one. Under such circumstances we would be better advised not to undertake the sort of study that we wish to.

The objection under consideration, however, would have been respectable had the situation been as it holds or even expects it to be. But, unfortunately, the prevalent situation is different. In spite of the fact that many scholars have attempted to study the nature and significance of Nāgārjuna's philosophical thought, the efforts under consideration have given rise to considerable difference of opinion and such a mass of variety of views about his philosophy has given rise to confusion and misunderstandings. As a result, it has become exceedingly difficult to see what precisely is his philosophical position. The matter has become worse confounded especially in so far as that sort of philosophical position that has been attributed to him is at variance from the one he, as a matter of fact, wishes to upheld and defend. Furthermore, very often than not a certain doctrine, a certain methodological or even a certain perspective itself has come, unfortunately, to be equated with his philosophical position. Moreover, a doctrine has come to be studied in isolation from the methodological tool—say, *Pratītya Samutpāda*—is studied in isolation from *Śūnyatā* or conversely or, methodological tool has been studied in isolation from the perspective—say, *Śūnyatā*—has been studied in isolation from *Nirvāṇa* or, further still, his philosophical position—*Madhymā Pratipad*—either nowhere finds its mention or is mentioned in isolation from *Pratītya Samutpāda*, *Śūnyatā* or *Nirvāṇa*. These are some of the prominent shortcomings of the extant studies in the philosophy of Nāgārjuna, though, by no means, are these the only shortcomings one can think of. Under such circumstances, interrelation between and among *Pratītya Samtupāda*, *Śūnyatā*, *Nirvāṇa* and *Madhyamā Pratipad* is either not at all articulated or where it is attempted to be articulated, it is far from being satisfactory. As a result, the basic conceptual framework of Nāgārjuna's philosophy has not at all been articulated or where an attempt in this direction has been made, it has remained ambiguous and frought with many inadequacies. This being the case, it has become enormously difficult to comprehend and understand the philosophy of Nāgārjuna, leave alone understanding its relevance and significance—contemporary or otherwise. Given this kind of situation prevalent in our intellectual atmosphere, the task of understanding Nāgārjuna's link with the teaching of the Buddha, though they were severed from each other by couple of centuries, has remained far from being clearly accomplished. It is this kind of situation, therefore, that prompted us to undertake the sort of study that we wish to with a view to formulate and articulate framework of Nāgārjuna's philosophy, leaving to future consideration the issue of studying its contemporary significance. This kind of limitation is brought in due to the fear of work becoming difficult to complete in certain time span. We grant, however, that an investigation on this line is also equally important and urgently called for.

Method of the Present Study

We said that our aim is to articulate the framework of Nāgārjuna's philosophy through studying interrelationship between *Pratītya Samutpāda*, *Śūnyatā*, *Nirvāṇa* and *Madhyamā Pratipad*. The last of these being Nāgārjuna's philosophical position the task that needs to be undertaken is to show that his philosophical position arises out of the interrelationship of the first three with *Madhyamā Pratipad*. In order to do this one must have to develop an understanding about Nāgārjuna's works. Of the number of works that are ascribed to Nāgārjuna not all, unfortunately, are available in *Sanskṛta*. Normally one has to rely upon those that are extant and fortunately available and among those which are available one has further to utilize those which are useful for the purpose at hand. Considering this way, of those works of Nāgārjuna which are available in *Sanskṛta*, two stand out very prominently, viz. *Madhyamakaśātra* and *Vigrahavyāvartani*. But from the point of view of an elaborate statement of the philosophical view of Nāgārjuna it is the former of them that is crucially important. This is not in any way to undermine or belittle the importance of other works. But the fact remains that anybody who wants to understand some of the principal tenets of Nāgārjuna's philosophy in a considerable details cannot afford to ignore the work under consideration. We have made an extensive use of *Madhyamakaśāstra*. We have, of course, given priority to Nāgārjuna's contention in the work under reference and have taken help from Candrakīrti, his commentator, wherever this kind of need arose. Other work of Nāgārjuna like *Vigrahavyāvartani*, *Ratnāvali* have also been relied upon wherever and to whatever extent it was possible and desirable to do so. The major point of concentration is, however, *Madhyamakaśāstra*. Here as well as in case of other works of Nāgārjuna we have relied upon the original works in *Sanskṛta* rather than their translations and summaries.

We have, thus, tried to remain as close to the original works of Nāgārjuna as was possible and desirable.

Brief Outline of the Study

In the first chapter we present an outline of the principal interpretations of Nāgārjuna's philosophy at the hands of various scholars and bring out some of the crucial difficulties they appear to give rise to.

Second chapter is addressed to formulation of the theory of *Pratītya Samutpāda* as Nāgārjuna understands it, wherein it is argued that it presents Nāgārjuna's world view, according to which discrete particular unique things alone are real and the only thing that is true of them is that they are connected though not necessarily causally.

The third chapter discusses the nature of Śūnyatā as a methodological tool employed by Nāgārjuna to arrive at a sort of nominalism and to weed out proliferative ontological, epistemological and linguistic abberations on our part. It is argued that employment of *Śūnyatā* at Nāgārjuna's hands does not and cannot give rise to nihilism.

In the fourth chapter we explain the nature of *Nirvāṇa* as a philosophical perspective which, according to Nāgārjuna, needs to be adopted with a view to arrive at a philosophical position called *Madhyamā Pratipad*. It is further argued that *Pratītya Samutpāda Śūnyatā* and *Nirvāṇa*, at the hands of Nāgārjuna are very intimately interrelated and to the extent to which one fails to understand the kind of interrelationship between them one is not likely to understand Nāgārjuna's philosophical position as he intends it to be taken. It is further pointed out that *Nirvāṇa* needs to be understood not so much as a summum bonum or bliss or an ethical or religious ideal to be accomplished but rather as a philosophical perspective and it is only when it is understood that way it can be taken to be a prominent pillar sustaining Nāgārjuna's philosophical position. It is further argued that thus understood alone it at once establishes connection with *Pratītyasamutpāda* and *Śūnyatā* on the one hand and *Madhyamā Pratipad* on the other. It is also pointed out that although *Nirvāṇa* as a philasophical perspective has ethical religious of social implications it is not, nevertheless, these which shape and structure it.

In the last chapter we argue that Nāgārjuna's philosophical position is not *Śūnyavāda* as it is often alleged but *Madhyamā Pratipad* and as a middle path it seeks to strike a via-media between nihilism and realism—the view according to which everything—real or imaginary—is real, or between eternalism and utter momentariness etc. Understanding Nāgārjuna's philosophical position in this way alone enables us to see its connection with Buddha's teaching, which otherwise remains vague and obscure, on the one hand, and with *Pratītya Samutpāda Śūnyatā* and *Nirvāṇa* on the other.

CHAPTER I
SOME VIEWS ABOUT NĀGĀRJUNA'S PHILOSOPHY AND THEIR IMPLICATIONS

Many scholars, Indian and Western, have paid enough attention to Buddhist philosophical thought in general and the tendency is ever increasing. Likewise a philosophical position of Nāgārjuna has also become the subject-matter of many scholarly investigations. Taking into account an important role Nāgārjuna played in the development of Buddhist philosophical thought, scrutiny of the kind is but a consequence of it. As a founder of the *Mādhyamika* school it is scarcely a wonder that many a scholars paid a close attention to his philosophy. Through such attempts number of perspectives came to be developed from which Nāgārjuna's philosophy came to be surveyed, discussed and explicated. Every attempt of this kind, however, by and large, endeavours to characterise Nāgārjuna's philosophical position in a certain way and comes to present its chief tenets in such a way that they will fit the characterization under consideration.

Classification of Perspectives about Nāgārjuna's Philosophy :

A survey of the different perspectives developed with reference to Nāgārjuna's philosophy will show that they readily fall into four main group : taking Nāgārjuna's philosophy as (A) Nihilistic (B) Monistic (C) Absolutistic and (D) Mystical in character. These perspectives are not limited to particular time of their first development and one can easily discern representatives of any of these perspectives scattered over various time and regions. It might, however, have been the case that a certain perspective was more predominant at a given time. This was not, nevertheless, in itself a very prominant reason that invited attention of scholars to Nāgārjuna's philosophical thought. In this chapter we hope to take a close look at these perspectives about Nāgārjuna's philosophy and point out, at the end, some of the important difficulties that they give rise to jointly or separately. Consideration of this kind, we hope, will pave a way for later exploration.

Upto the end of nineteenth and first half of the twentieth century there seems to have been an overwhelming verdict of scholars that *Mādhyamikas* were nihilist, irrespective of the persistent denial of Nāgārjuna and others to be known as such. (We hope to bring out this feature of Nāgārjuna's philosophy in the sequel.) Not only Indian scholars but some European scholars of repute as well considered to be authority in this area of Indian philosophical thought, were of the opinion that *Mādhyamikas* were nihilists. Prof. Kern, Keith, Poussin and Walleser are among them. Among Indian scholars like Hiriyanna and Dasgupta could not formulate other opinion and could be said to have come under the sway of the view held by the European scholars. This may perheps be due to the upper hand of historian over philosophers in them which seems to have inhibited them to think otherwise. Many of the modern scholars, though unanimous in not admitting *Mādhyamikas* as nihilists, exhibit a difference of opinion saying that *Mādhyamikas* are either monists or absolutists or sceptic or even mystics. Stcherbatsky, T.R.V. Murti, Radhakrishan and B.G. Ketkar[1] are among them. Before coming to formulate our own view regarding the nature of *Mādhyamika* Philosophy, it would perhaps be proper and desirable to consider what makes these scholars to uphold their respective strands about *Mādhyamika* philosophical thought in general and Nāgārjuna's philosophy in particular. Side by side we hope to sketch, in outline, the main arguments which prominent representatives of each of the strands marshalled in support of their contention.

(a) *Nāgārjuna's Philosophical Position is Nihilism* :

First of all, something about the term nihilism. Nihilism is a revolutionary doctrine that seems to have originated in the nineteenth century. It was more a revolutionary tendency denouncing existing moral, religious and social principles. But, although, in this way originally nihilism is not an epistemological or ontological theory, very soon a nihilist is required to embrace epistemological scepticism especially when he undertakes the task of explanation and justification of knowledge claims. Epistemological scepticism, in turn, soon culminates into methodological scepticism and when methodological scepticism is generalized and universalized such a sceptic is bound to be denouncing everything—ontological, epistemological or otherwise. In India and perhaps elsewhere nihilism came to be understood as such a global kind of scepticism specially in ontological and epistemological domains. This is how, perhaps, the term nihilism in philosophy came to signify the doctrine that nothing exists or is knowable or is satisfactorily communicable.

Sometimes, restrictedly, however, the term is used to denote a doctrine that moral norms cannot be justified by rational arguments. It is also widely used to denote a mood of dispair over the emptiness or triviality of human existence in general. There is likewise a tendency to associate it with Atheism. This means that the term has a wide connotation, in different spheres of human knowledge. When one thinks how this doctrine got the status of a school in philosophy one is disposed to recollect a famous thesis of sophists, particularly of Gorgias, that 'nothing exists'. Though sophists were not perhaps serious about the dictum, other scholars took it seriously. Gorgias was certain that 'nothing' is not a name of a special entity nor did he mix up the issue of grammatical subject with it. He was rather arguing simply apriorily, to point out the impossibility of maintainability of certain position. For instance, if there were anything, it would be either eternal or have come into being; but it cannot have come into being because neither out of being nor out of non-being can anything come to be. Nor can it be eternal. For, if it were eternal, it would have to be infinite. But infinite is impossible. Therefore, it would be nowhere. And what is nowhere is nothing. Hence nothing exists.

It is, indeed, in similar vein that *Mādhyamika* Buddhists in general and Nāgārjuna in particular came to be described as nihilists. The view that *Mādhyamika* position or that of Nāgārjuna is nihilistic might appear to be, at least *prima facie*, plausible on the following grounds : (a) There seems to be a similarity between the arguments of sophists and those of *Mādhyamikas*. As sophists assert that there exists nothing on logical ground similarly Nāgārjuna with his critical and destructive method disproves the thesis of his opponents. Examining the view of his opponents on number of occasions he endeavours to show that the kind of thesis they wish to uphold is untenable. If it is accepted, as is generally the case, that there is a cause, it produces an effect etc. a *Mādhyamika* like Nāgārjuna will argue that there is no cause, the thing is not produced by itself or by another or by both or by neither. The doctrine of causation must, therefore, be taken as referring only to the world of ignorance[2] (b) Similarly Nāgārjuna considers, on the line of sophists, that eternal and everlasting being is logically impossible. Various chapters of *Madhyamakaśāstra* are directed to consider critically various categories upheld by opponents and the ultimate end of Nāgārjuna in undertaking such an examination seems to prove that what is assumed by way of thesis by his adversaries is an utter impossibility on the logical ground. Prof. Keith points out that every conceivable relation yields to such a negative dialectic. Subject and object, action and actor, fire and fuel, characteristic and the thing characterised, sensation and perception etc. all these, including the Buddhist doctrines of *Tathāgata* etc., prove that they neither exist of themselves nor by others nor by both nor by neither.[3] Due to this similarity between sophists and *Mādhyamikas* as former are branded as nihilists, the latter too, came to be considered to be nothing else but nihilists. (c) It is often held that Nāgārjuna frequently considers the objects of our normal experience as the objects of illusion and hallucination and thus treats them as unreal.[4] Because of his persistent denial of a (fixed) 'thing' in this world scholars like Poussin, Keith, Kern hold a view that 'nothing is real' is the dictum of Nāgārjuna's nihilism.[5] (d) It is held that Nāgārjuna uses the term '*Śūnya*' to express the conclusion of his reasoning. His repeated use of the expression *Śūnya* and his seeming failure to explain the correct import of the expression seems to have led the scholars to create a confusion. Due to this, it appears, the term is understood at their hands in various senses. For instance, sometimes it means 'void', sometimes it means 'devoid of', sometimes it means 'devoid of the nature of one's own', while sometimes else it means 'unreal'.[6] Thus, taking *Śūnya* as that which does not have a nature of its own, equivalent to nothing has *svabhāva*, meaning thereby, nothing has a nature of its own, which ultimately is taken to boiling down to nothing exists on its own nature *Mādhyamikas* come to be lebelled as *Śūnyavādins* i.e. nihilists. The same trait is said to be exhibitted by Nāgārjuna's philosophy and accordingly it came to be characterised as nihilistic. (e) Concentrating on Nāgārjuna's method of proof of the things under consideration, by employing logically rigorous arguments, Indian scholars like Kumārila,[7] Vācaspati Miśra[8] and Śaṁkarācārya[9] condemned him as *sarvavaināsika* i.e. nihilist. It means Nāgār· juna rules out, even in principle, anything either to be existent or knowable internal or external. Prof. Keith remarks on this method of *Mādhyamikas* in general and on Nagarjuna's in parti- cular that due to its employment we cannot make really any affirmation regarding anything; 'all is mere appearence'.[10] (f) Kern points out that *Mādhyamikas* are complete nihilists for, (1) they teach that the whole of a phenomenal world is a mere illusion; (2) they recognise two kinds of truths *Paramārtha satya* and *Saṁvṛtti satya*, of which the second kind truth is a mere illusion or properly speaking no truth at all.[11] Similar opinion is expressed by La De V. Poussin.[12] He further says that Nāgārjuna pours notions of cause, knowledge, motion etc. into the model of four branched syllogism and shows that the production or generation of anything is logically impossible. Thus, on different grounds various scholars—ancient or modern, oriental or western —put forth the view that Nāgārjuna's philosophy is nihilistic and these are some of the points which, perhaps, seem to have led them to hold the view that Nāgārjuna advocated nothing else but nihilism.

Thus, in the eyes of those who considered Nāgārjuna to be a nihilist, he repudiates the reality of the whole world or at least denies reality of any phenomenally real thing. The view seems to have been reinforced not only by critics of Nāgārjuna like Śaṁkara but also by the fact that Nāgārjuna himself ques- tions veracity of some of the celebrated categories like causality, eternality etc. It remains to be seen whether and how far the view is supported by what Nāgārjuna says and the arguments he marshals in support of his contention.

(b) Nāgārjuna's Philosophy as Monism :

At the outset, let us briefly say something about monism. Monism is a philosophical theory which recognizes only a single kind of reality, whether physical or psychical, and thus the term is equally applicable to materialism as well as idealism. In the history of philosophy efforts have been sufficiently carried out to reduce these two dichotomous elements to either one or the other. In consequence, there arises a trend of bare materialism or bare idealism or any moderate camp between the two extremes depending upon the preponderance of either mind over matter or conversely. This doctrine, though originally restricted to the function and place of mind or/and matter in the ultimate analyis of human experience, later on it came to be developed into epistemological monism. Thus, as a revolt against materialism and subjective idealism, Hegel and his successors came to advocate 'Absolute Idealism' (sometimes known as objective idealism). It professed that the primary source of being is not the personal human mind but some objective or world consciousness, the 'Absolute Spirit' the 'universal reason' and it furnished a peculiar philosophical basis for religion. This is how, perhaps there is a passage from monism to absolute idealism.

When the question whether '*Mādhyamikas* are monist'[13] comes before us, it requires to spell out under what conditions one is led to draw this conclusion about *Mādhyamikas*. It is Stcherbatsky, who, for the first time, seems to have advocated the view that *Mādhyamika* philosophy is a monistic system. Disagreeing with the tradition in treating *Mādhyamikas* as nihilist he pointed out that Prof. Keith, Prof. Walleser and others have taken into account only negative side of Nāgārjuna's philosophy.[14] But if they would have considered positive counter-part of his negativism they would have, perhaps, like himself, come to uphold the view that Nāgārjuna advocated monism.[15] He further says that the influence of *Aupaniṣadic* tradition upon Buddhism in general and *Mahāyana's* Buddhism in particular is one of the reasons of its being monistic.[16] He identifies the so-called Buddhist concept of Cosmic Body (*Dharmakāya*) with *aupaniṣadic* and later on with the *Vedāntic* Concept of *Brahman*. As a corollary of such an identification he deduces the conclusion that as *Vedānta* philosophy is considered as a monistic system, so too, *Mādhyamika* philosophy is a monistic system. In support of his view he says that dialectic of Nāgārjuna was mainly directed against pluralism of *Vaibhāsikas* in order to establish the idea of the Cosmic Body of the Buddha.[17] He further adds that the aim behind the employment of dialectical method was to show illusoriness of commonly upheld categories, incompetence of reason and worthlessness of logic in the business of knowing such a reality. But these were, for Nāgārjuna, only peripheral issues. The main focus behind this view, says Stcherbatsky, was to establish the unique, indefinable essence of Being, the One without the Second.[18] He finds similarities between Nāgārjuna's system and other monistic system such as the system of Nicholas of Cusa or G. Bruno.[19] But, when Stcherbatsky found that such a monistic system is harmful so far as the religious part of the Buddhism is concerned, he started saying that there is an element of mystic experience in the *Māhyamika* philosophy.[20] He says, particularly in dialectic, where logic was denied altogether, a necessary preparation for the acquisition of the intended goal consisted in a course of negative dialectics, after which an intuition of the transcendental truth springs up as an inward conviction and there is a moment of sudden illumination.[21] This admittence of mystic experience as an ingredient in one's realization of the monistic principle at the hands of Stcherbatsky seems to indicate the impact of the concept of 'Absolute' upon him, where one notices a considerable influence of Hegel upon him. Borrowing an idea of absolute spirit from Hegel, on the line of Spinozistic monism, Stcherbatsky seems to provide a philosophical basis for Buddhism as a religion. This is how he shifts his view from monism to absolute idealism.

In this passage of Stcherbatsky from monism to absolute idealism, Stcherbatskian consideration of *Mahāyāna* Buddhism in general and *Mādhyamika* Buddhism in particular as a religion paves a way for certain concepts being understood more religiously rather than philosophically. This seems to have led to the reduction of philosophical importance of such concepts. For instance, *nirvāṇa* which is a philosophical concept, became a religious ideal to be achieved by everyone as a final deliverance or an absolute end. By showing certain similarities between Buddhism and other Indian systems with a conclusive opinion that there is no difference in the meaning of non-Buddhistic expressions such as '*Mokṣa*' or '*Apavarga*' and *nirvāṇa*,[22] he completely washed away the unique philosophical significance of the expression *nirvāṇa*. As a result of it he constantly uses an expression 'Absolute' in place of *nirvāṇa*. Thus he says : "with regard to *Nirvāṇa* or the Absolute, Indian philosophy is divided into two diametrically opposed solutions. The absolute end is either eternal death or it is eternal life. The first is materalism and the second is some kind of idealism. Both theories are represented in India by Buddhism as well as by Brahmanism. The theory of eternal death is represented on the side of Buddhism by early Buddhism and *Vaibhāṣikas* .....and the theory of eternal life is represented on the side of Buddhism by the *Mahāyāna* and its precursors".[23] In nutshell, one can paraphrase it thus : like non-Buddhist schools Buddhism also advocated the doctrine of the Absolute, To hold such a view means to make an allowance to some kind of idealism. Hence *Mahāyāna* in general and *Mādhyamika* in particular advocated Absolute idealism according to Stcherbatsky.

Thus, in the eyes of Stcherbatsky Nāgārjua seems to have advocated 'Absolute Idealism' by propounding the view that the whole world or a part thereof have their origin in absolute spirit that can be known only through mystic experience. Now it remains to be seen whether and how far the view is supported by Nāgārjuna. It will have, especially, to be shown, if the above view is to stand, that reality, according to Nāgārjuna is spiritual and that it is only one.

(c) *Nāgārjuna's Philosophy as Absolutism :*

Now something about Absolutism. Absolutism is a term coined sometime in the nineteenth or early twentieth centnry. The term signifies that the upholders of this school advocate that the notion of 'the Absolute' enjoys an exclusive significance so far as the philosophical discussion of the problem of (the nature of) ultimate reality is concerned. It holds the view that the ultimate referent or the terminus of thought in such matters is 'the Absolute'. This Absolute is eternal, unconditional, perfect, unchanging and complete in itself.[24] The term has variety of a significations. In the faculty of law the term signifies a form of government having no legal or moral limitations upon the power which they wield.[25] In religion, God is referred as 'the Absolute'. Fischte, Hegel, Bradley, Schelling are some of the thinkers who advocated absolutism and one can say that it is nothing but an expanded and modified version of Absolute Idealism. It stands for variety of metaphysical conceptions in the history of philosophy.[26] None the less, one can very easily notice that every absolutism is monism but not vice-versa. For, while absolutism of every kind seems to abhor pluralism, monism in itself necessarily does not. Within the framework of monism, for example, an allowance could be made for pluralism depending upon the perspective from which the reality is considered to be one and of a certain kind. If, for instance, it is taken to be material then we can have materialism leading to atomism. If, on the contrary, it is taken to be spiritual then we can have spiritual monism leading to Leibnizian monadism etc. In absolutism, however, generally speaking, that which is considered to be absolutely real is held to be, in some way or the other, spiritual in character. Thus that Absolutism that has been considered as idealism is often known as a form of monism. For it exalts the one over the many. Due to the similarities between this doctrine in exaltation of the one above everything and the mystical or religious belief it is associated with generally, it has often been described as a philosophical justification of monotheism.[27]

T.R.V. Murti, one of the prominent scholars of Buddhist philosophy, acknowledges the debt of Stcherbatsky in introducing new interpretation of *Mādhyamika* philosophy and thereby deviating from the then prevalent tradition. But at the same time he finds lacunae in Stcherbatskian interpretation. In consequence, in the preface of his book he says that his book is written to fill up the gaps that have been left behind by Stcherbatsky.[28] He widens the scope of Stcherbatskian Absolute from the concept of *nirvāṇa* to the concepts of *Śūnyata*, *dharmatā* and prajna and prefers to designate *Mādhyamika* philosophy as Absolutism.

Murtian consideration of the *Mādhyamika* philosophy mainly rests on the following points : (a) His interpretation of certain *Sanskrit* terms. (b) His notion of *Mādhyamika* dialectic, and (c) the Revolutionary character of *Mādhyamika* philosophy leading to what he calls Copernican revolution.

(i) Murti finds the evidence of *Mādhyamika* absolutism in the interpretation of 'Tattva' as a *Mādhyamika* definition of Reality. He interprets *Mādhyamika Kārikā* 9 Chapter XVIII thus : The Real is the *Absolute* self-conceived and self existent.[29] But by introducing a modification in the interpretation of the same *kārikā* at some other place[30] he tries to argue the *Mādhyamika* position saying that according to it the real falls outside

the Reason. It helped him to focus the difference in the interpretation of the Absolute by *Mādhyamikas* and other thinkers
and indirectly helped him show that *Mādhyamikas* are not in a
position to admit Hegelian equation 'Real is rational'.

(ii) He also designates the Absolute by an expression
'*Śūnya*'. While considering such an interpretation he seems to
have been influenced by Royce.[31] Thus, his line of thinking is
reflected in the following lines : "The *Absolute* is very aptly
termed as '*Śūnya*' as it is devoid of all predicates. The *Absolute*
is incommensurable and inexpressible. It is utterly transcendent
of thought."[32]

(iii) Murti does not understand dialectic in a usual sense as
a spiral process, series of triads where synthesis (at a higher
stage), of thesis and anti-thesis (at a lower stage), itself forms a
thesis for further dialectical operations. He finds such a process
as unending and is primarily governed by reason. He is, on the
contrary, of the opinion that for *Mādhyanikas* a dialectic is a
conflict of reason. It is self-conscious spiritual process, a cri-
tique of Reason. Further, he adds that it is in total conflict of
reason and also an attempt to resolve it.[33] To get rid of such a
conflict, says Murti, *Mādhyamika* rejects both the opposites
taken singly or conjunctively, for, reason is incompetent to comprehend the Reality. Thus, by employing dialectic as a weapon
in the form of reductio ad absurdum, *Mādhyamikas* disprove the
thesis under consideration they wish to repudiate. Murti points
out that there is just one triad of the *Mādhyamika* dialectic
(a) Dogmatism, i.e. speculative philosophy, (b) Transcendental
illusion which exposes the pretention of speculative reason and
reveals inner contradiction and (c) Criticism—the utter negation
of thought as revealatory of the real. Thus, he considers all
judgements, philosophical systems, as *vikalpas*, prapancas, false-
ascriptions or thought-constructions. *Mādhyamika* dialectics as
a negation of thought is intuition of the Absolute as uprooting
the passions. It is freedom and perfection as union with the
Perfect Being. Thus, dialectic as non-conceptual or intuitional
weapon takes us beyond the possibility of pain. It consummates
the union of all beings with the Perfect Being i.e. *Buddhakāya*.[34]

(iv) Fourthly, in the beginning Murti points out that the
Mādhyamika system is a revolution on various counts. In

Metaphysics it was revolution from radical pluralism to radical absolutism[35]......... In religion it was revolution from positivism to absolutistic Pantheism.[36] He points out that *advayavāda,* as a process of purification of the faculty of knowing, brushes aside the inveterate tendency to view Reality as one or many, momentary or permanent etc. and ultimately gives rise to Intuition i.e. *Prajñā, Tathatā, Dharmatā, Śūnyatā,* all these being synonymous expressions. Murti understands *Madhyamā Pratipad* as dialectical process by which philosophical consciousness, reaches intuition and remarks that *Mādhyamika Śūnyatā* can serve as the basis for a synthesis of all philosophical systems.[37]

(v) The notion *Śūnyatā* indeed plays a central role in the philosophy of the *Mādhyamikas.* As Stcherbatsky uses the word 'Absolute' for *nirvāṇa,* Murti repeatedly refers *Śūnyatā* by 'Absolute' and thereby recognizes *Mādhyamika* system as Absolutism.

(vi) Lastly, Murtian consideration of *Mādhyamika* system as a religion also matters in its being described as Absolutism. Though Murti earlier considers that *Mādhyamika* system is basically philosophical one, later on, some how, he makes an allowance to religious element to peep into the philosophical system of *Mādhyamikas.* Not only that, but going one step ahead he recommends that *Mādhyamika* religion should be considered as basis for world culture.[38] Thus, on the reciprocal relation we get *Mādhyamika* system as a Pantheism through religious glasses and such a Pantheism viewed through philosophical glasses gives rise to nothing else but Absolutism.

These are some of the points which led Murti to consider that *Mādhyamika* Philosophy is Absolutism. It still remains to examine Murti's stand on *Mādhyamika* system and how far it is supported by Nāgārjuna.

(d) *Nāgārjuna's Philosophical Position is Mysticism*

Lastly, let us consider mysticism. The term mysticism has its origin perhaps in the German word 'mystik' which stands for immediate divine-human relationship. The word, understanding it in a quite strict sense, implies an immediate, non-discursive, intuitive relation with the Absolute. It is used, by and large, as a form of religious experience. Though many thinkers have tried to define mysticism, the term has not yet been free of ambiguity. As a result of such an ambiguous nature, it is widely used in religion, poetry, philosophy, aesthetics etc. In the efforts of setting aside ambiguity of emotive meaning of the term and to understand it cognitively, two distinct uses of the term have been coined. In one sense, it has been used to refer to a tendency, an awareness, of a first-hand experience of the Divine, which is a psychological characteristic. In the second sense, it has been used to signify a theologico-metaphysical doctrine of such an unusual experience of a thinker.[39] In the present context we are concerned with the second sense.

Taking into account the possibility that such unusual experience of a person can be generalized, Russell enlists the following characteristic beliefs of such experience under the head of mystical philosophy.[40]

(1) There is a belief in insight as against discursive analytic knowledge—the belief in a way of wisdom, sudden, penetrating, coercive which is constrasted with the slow and fallible study of outward appearance by a science relying wholly upon the senses.

(2) Mysticism believes in unity and refuses to admit opposition or division anywhere.

(3) The third mark of mysticism is the denial of the reality of time.

(4) The last characteristic of mysticism is its belief that all evil is mere appearance.

The view that *Mādhyamika* system is not a philosophy but mysticism is propounded by Prof. B.G. Ketkar. It is mainly based upon the four characteristics mentioned above. In support of his contention he cites an evidence from Nāgārjuna's *Madhyamika Śāstra* which, according to him, exhibits the characteristics of mysticism mentioned above.

(a) According to Ketkar, Nāgārjuna distinguishes mysticism from philosophy and advocates rejection of philosophy. For instance : (i) persons of a meagre intellect, who nevertheless perceive existence and non-existences of things, do not realize the ultimate end, the blissful end of the perceptible world.[41] (ii) The wise have taught *Śūnyatā* to be the renunciation of all philosophical theories. They have further declared that those who understand *Śūnyatā* to be a philosophical theory are incurable.[42] (iii) Reality is not many and is devoid of a nature of its own. It can not be realized from the teaching of others. It is beyond the reach of mind and is inexpressible in language.[43] There are other *Kārikās*, too, which seem to boil down to the same meaning and, therefore, have been quoted in support of the point.[44]

(b)   Kārikās 33, 34 and 8 from the Chapter Nos. VII, XVII and XXIII respectively of *Madhyamaka Śāstra* whose second line is 'Gandharvanagarākārā marīci svapnasannibhaḥ' shows that Nāgārjuna was convinced of the unreality of the world.[45]

(c)   The entire chapter nineteenth of the *Madhyaka Śāstra* 'the examination of Time' is the evidence of Nāgārjuna's denial of the reality of Time.[46]

(d)   Nāgārjuna dissolves the distinction between good and evil through the following Kārikās : (i) How would anything be good or bad when these objects of experience are a creation of our fancy, like a person created by magic, like a reflection?[47] (ii) The evil, in relation to which we are trying to establish the good does not exist independently of the good. Hence nothing is good [48] Similarly, (iii) The good, in relation to which we are trying to establish the evil does not exist independently of the evil. Hence nothing is evil.[49]

One more point in support of his thesis of mysticism that Ketkar brings forward is that as a true mystic, Nāgārjuna must believe in a mystical way of understanding the reality. Likewise, he denounces all the other so-called valid sources of knowledge as they give rise to ignorance. This characteristic says Prof. Ketkar is reflected in the works of Nāgārjuna particularly when he refutes all sources of vaild knowledge and declares that all philosophical systems are futile.[50]

These are some of the points which seem to have led Prof. Ketkar to account *Mādhyamika* philosophy as a mysticism and thereby conclude that Nāgārjuna was a true mystic. The view seems to have been reinforced not only because of Nāgārjuna's stand about the nature of reality, time, evil etc. but also due to his consideration of the so-called validity of valid sources of knowledge. It remains to see how far the view is supported by Nāgārjuna's contention.

Important Difficulties Arising from these Interpretations :

As it has been already pointed out, these four main views about the philosophy of Nāgārjuna give rise to certain difficulties, which demand a legitimate clarification. Such a clarification may perhaps succeed in giving a new interpretation of Nāgārjuna's philosophy. In this section I would like to enlist some of the important difficulties that these interpretations seem to give rise to.

First of all the question is : granted, for the sake of argument, that Nāgārjuna advocated nihilism, it remains to spell out what sort of nihilism he wanted to cherish ? That is, does his position take him to profess utter nihilism or partial nihilism? Furthermore, does his nihilism ultimately take up to a form of scepticism ? And even if it is granted that he is sceptical about some questions, it still remains to point out the exact position of his scepticism. Secondly, one of the important reasons of considering the *Mādhyamika* philosophical position to be nihilism is its comparison with sophistry. But scholars seem to have ignored the very intention behind the procedure followed by the adherents of respective schools. Sophists, being teachers by profession experts in discussion, employed rhetoric as a means to win in discussion and debates. This being so, can one legitimately compare *Mādhyamika* with sophist saying that the intention behind the use of the method of reductio ad absurdum was the last resort for him to win in the discussion and to establish nothing ? Thirdly, it is held that Nāgārjuna uses the term *Śūnya* to express the conclusion of his reasoning. But, his repeated use of the term itself forms a special status of its being known as a philosophically technical term. Naturally, it is alleged, the philosophy of that particular thinker comes to be known by that technical term. Il is, nevertheless, interesting to note, as will be pointed out in the sequel, that Nāgārjuna does not characterise his philosophical position to be *Śūnyavāda*. It is the characterization of it at the hands of others. Hence, it needs to be inquired into as to whether and to what extent, if at all, that characterisation is tenable. But this was not the only intention of scholars when they say that *Mādhyamika* philosophy is *Śūnyavāda*. On the contrary, they say that when Nāgārjuna speaks of '*Śūnyatā*' it means either utter void or something synonymous to such an expression, and it led people to understand *Śūnyavāda* as nihilism. This being the case, it is necessary to spell out the import of the term '*Śūnya*' in the way in which Nāgārjuna uses it and also to point out whether it means nihilism.

The monistic, absolutistic, and mystical interpretations of Nāgārjuna's philosophy acknowledge, in one way or another, an upper hand of spiritual element over matter and an ultimate analysis the explanation boils down to religious rather than a philosophical explanation of his position. In the monistic and absolutistic interpretations, moreover, although philosophic aspect of Nāgārjuna's position is brought out, the idealistic and/or spiritualistic turn given to it needs to be examined afresh to see whether it is borne out by what Nāgārjuna has to say. Further, a question comes up at this stage that if Nāgārjuna does not seem to have discussed any problem with reference to religion in *Madhyamakaśāstra* then how far will it be right to consider his system primarily as a religious one ? Moreover, to say *Mādhyamika* system is monism or absolutism means to embrace some kind of extremism and it goes against Nāgārjuna's position that *Mādhyamika* school has sprung to avoid extreme positions of eternalism or annihilationism. Likewise, to say that *Mādhyamika* system is developed as a religion or as a basis of world culture amounts to assign such a role to it that seems at variance from its principal tenets. In a like manner, to say that Nāgārjuna's principal aim was to articulate a religious view amounts to rule out, almost apriorily, any differentiating role to it from that of the Councils, the principal aim of which was to formulate Buddha's religious teaching. Hence, it is necessary to probe into Nāgārjuna's major works with a view to see whether the consideration that *Mādhyamika* system is not a philosophy but a religion is tenable as also to find out whether this tenet is exhibited by Nāgārjuna as well.

When we come to the Murtian interpretation of Nāgārjuna's philosophy, the following questions need to be answered. (a) Murtian interpretation of the word '*tattva*' is so loose that it escapes the ontological import of it. Is it synonymous to *svalakṣaṇa* ? If so, it must be made clear. (Nāgārjuna himself does not employ the expression *svalakṣaṇa*). (b) Similarly, Murtian account of 'dialectic' seems to lack consistency. Some-

times the term signifies a process, sometimes it conveys the ultimate end-point of such a process. It therefore, is necessary to
find out what notion of dialectic, if any, is at stake in *Mādhyamika* system in general and in Nāgārjuna in particular.
(c) Murtian so-called copernican revolution, instead of giving
lucid interpretation of Nāgārjuna's philosophy many times
engenders paradoxes. It remains to be seen whether this kind of
paradoxicality is the tenet of Nāgārjuna's thought. (d) One of
the controversial issues regarding Murtian interpretation is his
designation of many things by the term 'Absolute'. It creates an
impression that his 'Absolute' is such an elastic and blanket
term that it covers anything under the sun and gives rise to proliferative ontology. Such points which arise while going through
Murti's book need to be reconsidered and it is required to be
seen whether they could be answered satisfactorily. Such an
attempt may perhaps lead to interpret *Mādhyamika* philosophy
differently.

Next difficulty arises about Prof. Ketkar's interpretation of
Nāgārjuna's philosophy. He is not willing to accept Nāgārjuna
as a philosopher; rather he treats him to be mystic. At this
stage the first question that arises is : are the characteristics,
which are mentioned in support of mysticism, necessary conditions to be fulfilled, to regard anyone to be a mystic ? Could it
not be a case that one may fulfil some of these conditions and yet
may not be a mystic ? For instance, Henri Bergson denies the
reality of time and yet he may not be considered to be a mystic.
And even if it is granted that Nāgārjuna is sceptical about some
problems such as reality of Time or reality of the world, that will
mean that one needs to elaborate his scepticism and not to take it
to be mysticism instead. Not only that, but considering *Mādhyamikas* as mystic seems to mean (1) that they admit and give due
importance to God and (2) they admit a mystic way as stepping
stone towards the kinship, that a being wants to establish with
this Divine i.e. God. But unfortunately neither Prof. Ketkar
evidently shows it to be the case nor does he quotes evidence
from *Madhyamakaśāstra* conducive to it. One more point is that
when one wants to study a system of a particular thinker, while
doing this if he is aware of the following points, viz. (i) the
impact of the then existing socio-religious, and cultural environ-
ment in which that particular thinker is brought up. (ii) The
technical terms that he uses frequently in his works. (iii) His

outlook about the language and its place in his philosophy, then he is likely to understand that thinker cogently and correctly. But Prof. Ketkar's attempt seems to be lacking on these points. Hence the question remains as to how far the interpretation given in acceptable.

In all these four attempts of characterising Nāgārjuna's philosophy, certain key-words seems to have failed to attract that sort of attention to them that they deserve. For instance, though Stcherbatsky and Murti give an account of *Pratītya Samutpāda*, its clearer import does not seem to have been brought out. Similarly, they seem to have failed to account for what *Madhyamā Pratipad* is ? Nāgārjuna often speaks of *Samvṛtti satya* and *Paramārtha satya* and in the light of these the attempts to draw a line of demarcation between *Samsāra* and *Nirvāṇa*. It becomes now incumbent upon us to clarify and study the distinction between these concepts, because, Nāgārjuna points out that those who do not understand the distinction between these two fail to understand the philosophy of the Buddha.[51] Besides, it is often held that according to Nāgārjuna 'nothing is real'. Therefore, it needs to be considered whether he has really said it and if so, what does it imply on the background of his own philosophic position ? Over and above all these problems one will notice that in this whole endeavour he seems to be more critical about certain kind of language and the sort of conceptual blemishes it paves way for. This problem again is two-fold. On the one hand, we have to consider language-knowledge relation. On the other hand, language-world relation needs to be given a closer look. Further it is necessary to take into account the role language plays in our whole endeavour of communication of reality.

The problems mentioned above are all important, no matter whether they arise from more than one perspectives about Nāgārjuna's philosophy or from a particular perspective. But it is not possible to deal with each one of them within the compass of the present work. To do something of this kind would be too ambitious a plan. Instead we propose to focus on the four principal issues : (1) First, we wish to state the theory of *Pratītya Samutpāda* with a view to trace the sources of some of the misunderstandings that have surfaced regarding it. But, apart from this negative side of the issue, we wish to bring out what sort of world does it seem to presuppose and why it cannot be considered to be a theory of causation ? (2) Secondly, we shall investigate extensively into the concept of *Śūnyatā* primarily to point out what positively and negatively is its import and how extensively Nāgārjuna wishes to understand it. But investigation of this sort will also be designed to point out whether and how far the interpretation of the concept at the hands of scholars is supported by what Nāgārjuna says or by what is implied by what he says. (3) Thirdly, we shall state the nature of *Nirvāṇa* as Nāgārjuna wishes to understand it and proceed to inquire whether it could be or is to be understood as a sort of ethical, religious or even mystical ideal. For, if *Nirvāṇa* is a perspective of the philosophic position we are commended to develop then it is necessary to inquire whether such a perspective needs at all to have an ethical, religious or even mystical anchorage. (4) Fourthly, we hope to state *Madhyamā pratipad* as a philosophical position of Nāgārjuna as he characterises it and brings out its implication. This is designed to be undertaken to be able to see whether and how far Nāgārjuna's philosophical position lends support to the kind of characterisation of it at the hands of different scholars, approaching the problem from different perspectives. This kind of investigation is necessitated by the need of understanding the focus from which Nāgārjuna is trying to solve or dissolve some philosophically important problems.

Thus, in the exercise that we hope to undertake we wish to concentrate on outlining the anatomical framework of Nāgārjuna's philosophy, setting aside all the peripheral issues, however important they might be. We shall argue that the philosophic position of Nāgārjuna—*Madhyamā Pratipad* as he calls it—rests on three principal pillars : *Pratītya, Samutpāda, Śūnyatā* and *Nirvāṇa*, which are mutually interrelated. Hence, an endeavour to understand any one of them in isolation from the rest two is misleading. This sort of attempt would also not enable us to understand Nāgārjuna's philosophic position as he is at pains to make us understand. But, we shall argue, that in so far as one's understanding of any one of these pillars of Nāgārjuna's philosophy is confused and muddled there is just no hope of one's coming to comprehend his philosophic position, too, in the proper perspective it endeavours to put before us. To be able to present, therefore, the skeleton of Nāgārjuna's philosophy one has to probe into three pillars of it and sketch out his philosophic position in the light of interconnection between its three pillars. To be able to accomplish this aim, one should begin an inquiry from *Pratītya Samutpāda*. This is not again arbitrary as it may *prima facie* appear. Nāgārjuna himself deals with it in the opening chapter of his treatise—*Madhyamakaśāstra*. We shall follow him. For, other things being equal, it seems to be the best alternative to understand the chief thrust of his argument. In the next chapter, therefore, we proceed to study *Pratītya Samutpāda* and bring out its prominent philosophical implications.

NOTES

1. Ketkar, B.G., *Nāgārjuna : A Fresh Study* : University of Poona; Ph. D. Thesis (unpublished).
2. Keith, A.B., *Buddhist Philosophy in India and Ceylon*, p. 238.
3. *Ibid*, p. 239.
4. *Madhyamakaśāstra*; 7.33, 17.34; 23.8.
5. Stcherbatsky, Th., *The Conception of Buddhist Nirvāṇa*, p. 43.
6. Ketkar, B.G., *Nāgārjuna : A Fresh Study*, University of Poona, Ph.D. Thesis (unpublished), p. 16.
7. Kumārila; *Ślokavārtika* 3:10:115; (cf) Radhakrishnan, S., Indian Philosophy, Vol. I, p. 651.
8. Stcherbatsky, Th., *The Conception of Buddhist Nirvāṇa*, p. 142 (footnote) No 9.
9. Śaṁkara; *Brahmasūtrabhāṣya* 2:2, 18-19.
10. Keith, A.B., *Buddhist Philosophy in India and Ceylon*, p. 239.
11. Kern, H., *Manual of Indian Buddhism* (Encyclopaedia of Indo-Aryan Research), p. 127.
12. Poussin, La De. V. *Philosophy (Buddhist)* (ERE) Vol. IX, pp. 848-49.
13. Stcherbatsky Th. *Conception of Buddhist Nirvāṇa*; p. 70 and many other places, Also, *Buddhist Logic*. Vol. I, p. 199.
14. *Ibid*, p. 60.
15. *Ibid*, p. 60.
16. *Ibid*, p. 59.
17. *Ibid*, p. 55.
18. *Ibid*, p. 55
19. *Ibid*, p. 62.

20. *Ibid*, p. 62.   Also *Buddhist Logic*, Vol. I, p. 63.

21. *Ibid*, p. 21.

22. *Ibid*, p. 63.

23. *Ibid*, p. 30.

24. Runes, D.D., *Dictionary of Philosophy*, p. 2.

25. *Collier's Encyclopaedia*, Vol. I, p. 30.

26. The Encyclopaedia of Philosophy, *Monism & Pluralism*, Vol. V, p. 363.

27. *Collier's Encyclopaedia*, Vol. I, p. 29.

28. Murti, T.R.V., *The Central Philosophy of Buddhism*, preface, p. viii.

29. *Ibid*, p. 139.

30. *Ibid*, p. 228.

31. *Colliers's Encyclopaedia*, Vol. I, p. 34.

32. Murti, T.R.V., *The Central Philosophy of Buddhism*, p. 236.

33. *Ibid*, p. 126.

34 Murti, T.R.V., *The Central Philosophy of Buddhism*, p. 142.

35. *Ibid*, p. 5.

36. *Ibid*, p. 6.

37. *Ibid*, p. 142.

38. Murti, T.R.V., *The Central Philosophy of Buddhism*, p. 337.

39. ERE, '*Mysticism*', Vol. IX, pp. 83.

40. Russell, B., *Mysticism and Logic*; pp. 8-11.

41. Ketkar, B G.; *Nāgārjuna : A Fresh Study* : Ph.D. Thesis, University of Poona, p. 130.

42. *Ibid*, p. 130.

43. *Ibid*, p. 130.

44. *Madhyamakaśāstra*; Kārikās 18.9; 24.40: 25.3 and 27.29-30.

45. *Ibid*, pp. 132-133.

46. *Ibid*, p. 133.

47. *Ibid*, p. 134.

48. *Ibid*, p. 134.

49. *Ibid*, p. 134.

50. *Ibid*, p. 113.

51. *Madhyamakaśāstra*, 24.9.

CHAPTER II

PRATĪTYASAMUTPĀDA

Three Perspectives about Change and Continuity

Ever since the dawn of human civilization two features of the world, viz. change and continuity, have occupied man's attention in one way or the other. There arise two principal issues about this kind of investigation : (i) Are these features of the world structural or otherwise and on what basis shall we be in a position to certify our claim, whatever it may be; and (ii) on what level of our enquiry do we satisfactorily attempt to account for these features of the world-pre-scientific, scientific or philosophical? On the count of each one of these issues there will naturally arise a very fundamental kind of difference of opinion. It is further no wonder likewise, that there will also be a very crucial difference between these different modes of accounting for the features of the world under consideration.

Consider, for example, the first issue of them. Suppose, further, that change and continuity are considered to be the structural features of the world. But, unfortunately, making this kind of assumption in itself drives nowhere. For, as soon as we have made such an assumption, host of problems crop up, like a jack in the box, some of which are : why do we make such an assumption under consideration? On what basis do we make it? Is it tenable? If so, on what ground/s? Unless and to the extent to which we shall be in a position to answer such questions warrantably, our assumption will have no intellectual foundation which it so desparately needs, if it is to have respectability. Suppose, further, that our assumption is tenable in a respectable way. Even then, however, we are not out of trouble. For, some different kind of problems beckon our attention. Consider, for instance, that continuity is a structural feature of the world and, perhaps, justifiably so. There, now, arise such [further problems as : Granted that the world is continuous, what kind of world are we talking about, of which continuity is a structural feature? On what basis are we in a position to certify our claim? Granted, further, that continuity is a structural feature of a certain world and that too justifiably so. Nevertheless, there arises another complicated problem : under what conditions can a world have continuity as a structural feature of it? Are they necessary or sufficient? If so, on what ground? Further, granting that world is continuous, does it mean that everything that belongs to it has to have this feature structurally as well? If something or even none of them has such a structural feature, is it just well-high impossible, even in principle, that the world still may have such a feature? In other words, granting that the world is continuous, has this continuity to be necessarily understood distributively as well?; or can the fact be different from this?

As we had a recipe of the kind of problems that arise with regard to our account of continuity as a feature of the world, likewise, it would be instructive to take a sketchy overview of the kind of problems we would be required to face in our endeavour to account for change as a feature of the world. Issues regarding assumption that world is continuous or changing are essentially similar; viz. why do we make the assumption, on what basis etc. But other sort of issues regarding change as a feature of the world, too, cannot be treated lightly, as it may appear feasible *prima facie.* For, it can equally partinently be asked : Granted that the world is changing, on what basis do we say so? Is our ground tenable? Is change as a feature of the world to be understood distributively? Granted that things belonging to the world change, how rapidly must they change? Must the change under consideration occur because of us or independently of us? Further, should the change arise because things are related to one another in a certain way or otherwise? No sooner we begin to inquire deeper and deeper host of such progressively complicated problems begin to cloud our understanding and make an otherwise simple-looking problem inextricably complicated.

When we turn to the second sort of issues the picture that emerges does not remain, unfortunately, simpler either. For, a common man or layman, a scientist and a philosopher may in their characteristic different ways, attempt to account for these features of the world. Consider a layman's approach. He attempts to account for these features on the basis of his experience of the world and things in it. Neither his experience nor understanding anchored in it are necessarily infected by scientific or philosophic modes of accounting for these features. His approach may, therefore, be characterised as pre-scientific one. This is not to say that in an advance state of civilization and culture scientific and/or philosophic modes of accounting for these features do not at all infiltrate common man's mode of accounting for them. But even when they do, on layman's level they often function and operate an undigested intellectual illumination and quite often lead to diarrhoea of words. That is why this kind of infiltration often engenders confusion rather than paving a way for clarity. Be that as it may. The crucial point, however, to note is that even a layman, in his own way endeavours to account for change and continuity as features of the world and his account often lacks credibility—scientific or philosophic. His account of these features is pre-scientific and experiential. This much characterisation of layman's account of these features of the world is enough for our present purpose.

Turning to philosophic account of these features, in an important sense philosopher's business may be said to be an attempt to try to make sense out of or interpret our experience of the world and/or things in it, ourselves, as also other beings—human as well as non-human. On this account it is of profound significance to bear in mind that our experiences of the above kinds vary-no matter whether those of which they are experiences so vary or not—and likewise our interpretations of them too vary—no matter, further, whether our experiences remain unchanged or not. Accordingly, even on the level of philosophic endeavour of accounting for change and continuity as features of the world there is every likelihood of there being plurality of views—often opposed to one another. The issue of philosophic account of these features becomes further complicated according as it converges or does not converge upon layman's account. In the former case, the philosophic account under consideration comes to be considered to be commonsensical and thus gains respectability even in the circle of layman. Where this fails to happen, there is, atleast initially, a resistence on the part of layman to accept it to be respectable, though in course of time it may gain respectability and thus may percolate even in layman's account of these features. But as remarked earlier, when this happens it operates largely as undigested intellectual protein for a common man. Similar convergence between philosophic and scientific accounts of these features of the world might be the case. When such turns out to be the case philosophic account may get respectability even within scientific circle. Where this kind of convergence arises with the proviso that philosophic account is chronologically prior, it is often held to be thematic precursor of science. Where, on the contrary, it is the scientific account that has chronological precedence over philosophic account, generally in such circumstances, philosophy comes to be considered scientific and thereby gains respectability not only in philosophic but also in scientific circles.

Coming to the scientific account. A scientist accounts for any feature of the world on the basis of examination and study of facts as they are presented in the light of a theory. In this endeavour he may come to be aided and helped by more and more sophisticated and progressively refined instruments with the help of which he may be enabled to fathom into the deeper and deeper structure and constitution of facts. On the basis of such profounder information older scientific accounts came to be enriched or replaced by new ones altogether. Thus, even in scientific knowledge there may not and often is not constancy. In fact, such a kind of fallibility is considered to be a hallmark of scientific knowledge. Be that as it may. It is not our present concern to probe deeper into this issue. It is noteworthy, again, that scientific and commonsensical or scientific and philosophic accounts might converge. But this is not a necessary precondition of its respectability. This is how, in many instances, members of above circles are at variance from each other.

As at any time, whatever the cruder or refined level of them, such three principal kinds of accounts of the above-mentioned features of the world are possible to be given, so too, was it the case in Buddha's or Nāgārjuna's times. But since at that time—especially at Buddha's time—the advancement of scientific knowledge was considerably meagre—as is evident from our knowledge of the history of the time—we need hardly to linger to ask : what might have been the scientific account of change and continuity as features of the world at Buddha's or Nāgārjuna's times. Eliminating, therefore, this mode of accounting for these features of the world there remain two—viz. commonsensical and philosophic. And like any other concerned and conscentious philosopher the Buddha, too, might have endeavoured to give a philosophic account of these features. In this attempt he might have come to differ from the then prevalent commonsensical as well as philosophic accounts of them at the hands of layman and philosophers of his time. He might have formulated his philosophic account, marshalled arguments in its support, critically examined similar such accounts at the hands of philosophers of the era and so on. But, unfortunately, since he did not commit anything to writing, after his demise there must have arisen a deep felt need to formulate Buddha's views on the subject. Many might have leaped and ventured. But from the history we learn that quite a few failed in their advanture, while only a few succeeded, but not without giving rise to difference of opinion. Thus, on the count of accounting for change and continuity to be the features of the world even at the time of Nāgārjuna there seems to be two principal kinds of accounts that were in vogue : commonsensical and philosophic. The latter of these were again of two main kinds : Those put forth by Buddhists and those by non-Buddhists. Each one of the former of these masqueraded as a genuine and authentic account of the features of the world under consideration as the Buddha wanted to put forth. Under such circumstances, Nāgārjuna's responsibility seems to be threefold : (i) To put forth what according to him is the view of the Buddha on the subject in a systematic way, (ii) to point out agreement with and differences from the then prevalent other philosophic accounts of these features—both the Buddhist and the non-Buddhist—and justify his claim as to why what he considers to be the Buddha's view on the matter is reliable, and (iii) to bring out the extent and the way in which the account he is presenting agrees with or differs from the commonsensical account of these features of the world and why the latter is not, when philosophically considered, tenable. It is some of these issues that appear to occupy Nāgār-juna's attention in his discussion of *Pratītya Samutpāda*. And since clearer understanding about them is so crucial to the development and explication of the philosophic position he endeavours to put forth in his *Madhyamakaśāstra*, he attempts to commence his treatise with a detailed consideration of *Pratītya Samutpāda*. As pointed out in the previous chapter, there being no special reason to depart, we shall follow him. For additional clarification we shall also keep ourselves informed and illumined, wherever necessary, by his commentator Candrakīrti.

Candrakīrti's Importance

Nāgārjuna in his *Madhyamakaśāstra*, does not appear to cite any quotation from the works of his predecessors or even contemporaries—Buddhist or otherwise. But this does not mean that he was ignorant of the Canons and canonical literature. In fact, Candrakīrti tells us that the work that Nāgārjuna undertook was not in isolation from or difference with the canonical literature. Rather, Nāgārjuna was helped considerably in producing the work that he did through his penetrating study of the texts like *Prajñāpāramitā*, *Laṅkāvatara* etc.[1] Though segregated from Nāgārjuna by couple of centuries, this testimony of Candrakīrti need not be doubted. Candrakīrti, too, in his turn, in his attempt to elaborate and explain the view of Nāgārjuna, not only draws upon canonical literature, citing relevant quotations, but also upon his predecessors. On the latter count he mentions their names, presents summaries of their views as also cites quotations from their works. This trend he follows through the entire treatise of his—*Prasannapadā*—with a view to reinforce, testify, clarify and elaborate the views of Nāgārjuna on different problems, of which *Pratītya Samutpāda* is just one. But his mentioning of works and authors posterior to Nāgārjuna but prior to him appears to be significant in an important way. Nāgārjuna has criticised his predecessors and contemporaries without mentioning anybody by name. Candrakīrti brings in the views of scholars posterior to Nāgārjuna with perhaps two motives : (a) to show that the view of those scholars which are in agreement with Nāgārjuna's are corroborative of Nāgārjuna's views, and (b) to show that the views of those scholars posterior to Nāgārjuna which are similar to those of Nāgārjuna's *Pūrvapakṣins* also stand opposed to and criticised by Nāgārjuna in anticipation. We made this point with a view to bring out important tenets of Nāgārjuna's thought : (a) one, his work is not an exercise in vacuum and undertaken in isolation from and with utter disregard to the Buddhist canonical literature—by far the first attempt to codify Buddha's philosophical teaching, and (b) secondly, the fact that Nāgārjuna criticises the views of Buddhist scholars should not be taken to be indicative of his total disregard for their views, whatever they might have said. He, rather, appears to be in agreement with them to the extent to which their views, in his judgement and considered opinion, could have been taken to be correct representation of Buddha's views on the matter. Further, according to Candrakīrti the rightness or Nāgārjuna's views appears to be corroborated by post—Nāgārjuna Buddhist scholars as well. Even if one leaves this out of consideration, the fact remains, as shown by Candrakīrti, that number of passages from the Buddhist canonical literature corroborate Nāgārjuna's views. We need not dwell further on this point.

Purpose of Madhyamakaśāstra

Though Nāgārjuna himself does not appear to tell us explicitly, at the outset, the purpose of his writing the treatise—*Madhyamakaśāstra*, his commentator Candrakīrti does not remain silent on the issue. He tells us that there are two principal objectives of his endeavour : first, to demarcate *neyārtha* and *nītārtha sūtras* (from canonical literature), and secondly, to bring out their respective imports as also to explain inter-connection between the two [2] He further tells us that those passages which are indicative of the proper mode (of investigation and enquiry) to be undertaken are known as *neyārtha*, as such a kind of enquiry alone can be said to be leading to the advent of the intended goal of philosophic illumination, while those which are instrumental to freeing us of our bewitchment through misleading impressions, confused concepts, ambigious language and platonistic world-view are said to be *nītārtha*.[3] The latter, further, are not supposed to produce that kind of comprehension on our part which arises when we come out of the above mentioned kind of bewitchment that we generally are prone to fall a prey to.[4] It is under the latter that the two major problems in Nāgārjuna's philosophy fall, viz. *Pratītya Samutpāda* and *Śūnyatā*, which will occupy our attention in this and the next chapter respectively. The two further issues, viz. *Nirvaṇa* and *Madhyamā Pratipad* that we will be dealing with in the fourth and fifth chapters fall under *neyārtha*. Of them, the *nītārtha* part is dealt with first by Nāgārjuna, though this is told to us by his commentator and not by Nāgārjuna himself, because of two reasons : first, *Nītārtha* will not dawn upon anybody so long as he continues to be bewitched otherwise by the kind of misunderstandings the *neyārtha* is supposed to do away with.[5] Secondly, both the aspects of canonical literature are dealt with in this way not only because they together are said to generate the requisite kind of philosophic understanding and comprehension but also because they are supposed to help us in doing away with the errors that may otherwise continue to mislead us.[6] Thus, the order in which Nāgārjuna has come to deal with the fundamental problems in his philosophy does not appear to be arbitrary. Rather, it is supported by the Buddhist canonical literature as also is fortified by cogent arguments. This information takes away much of the aura of arbitrariness that may otherwise come to be associated with Nāgārjuna's treatment of the problem.

Prevalent views about Pratītya Samutpāda :

Coming, thus, then to the *Pratītya Samutpāda.* As remarked earlier, the doctrine of *Pratītya Samutpāda* is developed with a view to present a philosophical account of change as a feature of the world. It is often held that when philosophers attempt to account for change as a feature of the world they come to present some or the other kind of theory of causation, holding in turn that any philosophically interesting change has to be causal. It is further argued, that as the Buddha was concerned with giving account of such a feature of the world, in presenting the theory of *Pratītya Samutpāda* he intended to put forth a causal theory and thereby account for the causal relatedness of things that belong to the world. Accordingly, those who hold the view under consideration understand the very expression *Pratītya Samutpāda* in the sense of 'Theory of Causation'[7] 'the formula of causal relations',[8] 'casual genesis',[9] etc., or that according to them the Buddha wanted to convey, through it, the view that the things in the world have only a 'dependent origination'.[10] Though no one denies that the doctrine is centrally situated in the philosophical geography of Buddhism yet it has been interpreted differently by the followers of Buddhism. But, non-Buddhist scholars, too, have contributed their mite and added fuel to the fire of already prevalent misunderstanding about it. At the hands of *Mādhyamikas* in general and Nāgārjuna in particular, however, as we shall see in the sequel, it gets a novel interpretation, and it is precisely here that its distinction lies.

Some of the modern scholars have attempted to present what, in their view, is the acceptable interpretation of *Pratītya Samutpāda.* But as we shall see, their attempts in this direction appear to create more problems than they solve. Theodore Stcherbatsky, for instance, appears to have understood, perhaps for the first time, the expression *Pratītya Samutpāda* in the sense of dependent origination.[11] For, every point instant of reality, according to him, arises in dependence of a combination of point instants to which it necessarily succeeds. That means, it arises in functional dependence upon totality of causes and conditions which are its immediate antecedents.[12] He arrives at the theory of dependent origination with the help of three formulas which are frequently used in the Buddhist literatuae and accepted as being preached by the Buddha in connection with his account of change and causation. They are : (a) This being that appears (b) There is no real production but only interdependence and, (c) All elements are forceless.[13] Though Stcherbatskian interpretation of *Pratītya Samutpāda* marked it off from the other interpretations of it at the hands of post-Nāgārjuna adherents of the various schools or Buddhism that came in vogue, yet he cannot be said to have done justice to the position of Nāgārjuna as it is presented in *Madhayamakaśāstra*. We shall present it in the sequel.

Later on, Stcherbatsky modified his view on *Pratītya Samutpāda* in his later writings. Particularly in his book 'The Conception of Buddhist Nirvāna' the doctrine has been interpreted as the painciple of Relativity.[14] But this interpretation, too, is also not free from misunderstanding and confusion, as we shall see. For, such a kind of relativistic interpretation is repudiated by Nāgārjuna himself. T.R.V. Murti, also like Stcherbatsky, diagnoses that *Pratītya Samutpāda* is not a law of causation. It can neither be regarded as a principle of temporal sequence as well. In his view it is the principle of essential dependence of things upon one another.[15] Thus understood, it turns out to be a theory of mutual dependence of things. Even other thinkers of Indian origin like Radhakrishnan did not point out any fundamentally divergent opinion from that of the Stcherbatskian tradition.[16] It is needless to say that there is a world of difference between the interpretation of *Pratītya Samutpāda* at the hands of modern scholars on the one hand and what Nāgārjuna intends to say through it on the other. But a glance of some of the prominent modern interpretations appears to be necessary with a view to see what sort of difficulties such (mis) interpretations are most prone to give rise to. This kind of understanding of them will also pave a way for us to consider the view of Nāgārjuna regarding *Pratītya Samutpāda* and see why modern interpretations of it are unsatisfactory.

Difficulties arising out of the interpretation of the docrine of Pratītya Samutpāda as a causal theory

The interpretation of the doctrine of *Pratītya Samutpāda* in terms of causation is not only at variance of the teaching of the Buddha but it totally fails to describe the nature of the world and things in it, for which it is originally preached by him. This being the case the first question that arises is : Is *Pratītya Samutpāda* intended to be understood as a law of causation? If so, between and among what kind of things is it supposed to be operative? On what basis is such a law sought to be established and warranted? Does this not presuppose a certain epistemological framework and what is the relation of it with the world as it is given to us? Is *Pratītya Samutpāda* intended to explain the coming to be and passing away of things in the world? Is the law under consideration derived from or based upon a very common confusion and a failure in making distinction between sequence and consequence[17] as Hume pointed out? *Pratītya Samutpāda,* at the most can be said to be the law of sequence, but can it also be said to be the law of consequence?[18] Secondly, does regarding *Pratītya Samutpāda* as a law of causation not presuppose certain metaphysical framework? Then, on what basis is it sought to be established? Granted that there is such a basis, how is one to make sense of and understand the fact that the Buddha refrained from formulating any metaphysical view and instead devoted much of his time and intellectual energy to cleanse up the then existing philosophical atmospher, which was clouded by many metaphysical and other theories including the thory of causality? This work, Nāgārjuna further carries out in the *Madhyamakaśāstra* by attempting refutation of most of the then prevalent metaphysical theories and side by side also showing how certain commonly cherished views are untenable. In this kind of endeavour of his he also exposes shortcomings, pitfalls in many of the possible causal theories. He repudiates self-causation, external causation and any other theory arising out of their combination. Did he carry out this exercise to substitute the then prevalent causal theories by the one he intended to put forth? Was it hoped to be matched with the kind of world we commonly hold to be given to us? If so, on what grounds can this be said to be acceptable? If *Pratītya-Samutpāda* is to be understood as a theory of dependent origination than is it to be understood in the sense that things that belong to the world depend upon prior things only for their origination? Are we, then, to suppose that like organisms in general and human beings in particular the originated things continue to be, other things being equal, independent of the things from which they originate, as organisms or human beings do, once they are born? If so, then, are we not using a kind of organismic or at least anthropo-centric model of the world? If we are, was it this that was expected to be done by Nāgārjuna? If so, on what grounds can one hope to universalize this and accept it as a philosophically satisfactory account of things? How can, likewise, it be said that such an account is a causal account of them? Relativity inter-pretation, likewise, does not appear to fare well. For, even if it is granted that things that belong to the world have a relative stability and are disposed to change frequently, it does not follow that the change under consideration must be a causal one and that *Pratītya Samutpāda* was put forth to advance a causal theory of such relatively stable things. Thus, in understanding *Pratītya Samutpāda* to be a theory of causation, in whichever form it is attempted to be understood, appears to create many problems than it solves. It is, therefore, not going to be helpful to try to understand *Pratītya Samutpāda* through the prism of any already available interpretation of it with a view to gain better insight iuto it. Instead, it would be better to probe into what Nāgārjuna has to say on the matter. So we turn to Nāgārjuna and his commentator Candrakīrti.

Meaning of Pratītya Samutpāda :

Before turning to outline Nāgārjuna's view regarding *Pratītya Samutpāda* it is necessary to pay attention to the semantical aspect of the expression. Though Nāgārjuna himself does not embark upon the task of explicating the meaning of the ex-pression '*Pratītya Samutpāda*', his commentator Candrakīrti pays enough attention to the problem. From this it appears that at the time of Nāgārjuna the significance of the expression might be fairly well-known and should be available readily in the then prevalent intellectual atmosphere. But with passage of time such an understanding of the expression must have gone becoming progressively hazier and through the fog of misunderstanding and variously interpreting it the expression must have come to raise considerable controversy and difference of opinion. Thus, during the time between Nāgārjuna and Candrakīrti the very significance of the expression *Pratītya Samutpāda* must have raised considerable dust of variant interpretations of it right in the Buddhist camp. As a result, there must have also arisen a problem as to which of them was meant by or is at least akin to Nāgārjuna's interpretation of it. Though Candrakīrti does not mention anybody by name, he, nevertheless, discusses four major modes of understanding the expression. He discusses them with a view to bring out that kind of significance of it that is consistent with Nāgārjuna's philosophical position. He begins the discussion of the problem of the significance of the expression with the *prima facie* most obvious of them all. The different ways in which the expression *Pratītya Samutpāda* could be understood, according to him, are : (i) To begin with, the expreesion *Pratītya Samutpāda* is a compound (expression) and is composed of two component expressions : (a) *Pratītya* and (b) *Samutpāda*. The former of them, in turn, is itself a compound expression formed out of 'prati' + 'itya', and 'itya', which is a *lyabanta*, together with *prati* is indicative of expectation (*apekṣā*) [19]   The expression *samutpāda* is formed by applying prefixes 'sam' + 'ut' to the verb 'pata' which together means emergence.[20] Hence, the entire expression means emergence of *bhāvas* (states of things) on account of (our) expectations (regarding them). This way of understanding the significance of *Pratītya Samutpāda* takes it to be a theory of the emergence of states of things through our expectations of them, not because things have dispositions to assume such states. (ii) Secondly, others contend,[21] interpreting '*itya*' in the expression *Pratītva* in the sense of annihilasion or destruction, that *Pratītya Samutpāda* is a theory of the emergence of the impermanent (*vināśinām*) objects that we experience. Thus, understood, they hold, the theory has to be held to be about what we perceptually experience—viz. our own private and non-shareable experiences (*vijñānam*).[22] But according to Candrakīrti, the expression *Pratītya* not being intended to be understood in

this but rather in former sense, the interpretation under consideration is untenable.[23]   In other words, the theory is not to be
understood as a theory of experiences that we have but rather of
states that things have. (iii) Thirdly, it is held that expectation
that leads to the advocacy of the theory of *Pratītya Samutpāda*
need not necessarily be tied with our experiences as is alleged to
be done in the second view discussed above.   Instead, it could be
taken to be combined with merely a possible experience.   Thus
understood, it can be said to be a theory of emergence of different
expectations (originating from their being) connected with possible experiences.[24]   Understood in this way, *Pratītya Samutpāda*
turns out to be a theory of the emergence of our expectations
rather than of experiences as is held under the second view.   But,
according to Candrakīrti, this view, too, is unsatisfactory.   For,
it creates two difficulties : First, granted that *Pratītya Samutpāda*
is a theory of emergence, is the emergence to be understood
generally or as emergence of something specific?   If the first, it
is needless to be connected with experience; if the latter, then
merely possible experience will not do.[25]   In fact the theory of
Pratītya Samutpāda is a philosophical theory and would hold no
matter whether it is corroborated by facts or not.   That is,
Pratītya Samutpāda is a theory of emergence of states of things
through our expectations of them, no matter our expectations
originate from experience or not—possible or actual.[26]   For, as
we shall show in the sequel, the theory of *Pratītya Samutpāda* is
not intended to tell us that what thus comes to be said to have
emerged is a fact philosophically speaking, but rather that it is
not a fact of this kind and hence cannot be real in the strict sense
of the term. This is the view that Nāgārjuna begins his investigation with.[27]   (iv)   Fourthly, it can also not be held that *Pratītya
Samutpāda* is a demonstrative theory of the emergence of each
one of the things.   For, first, such an over-ambitious programme
cannot even in principle be carried out.   But, secondly, the
theory is to be understood non-specifically and generally.[28]
Likewise, it can also not be held that the theory of *Pratītya
Samutpāda* is to be understood commonsensically, conventionally
and unsophisticatedly.[29]   For the very hypothesis that Nāgārjuna
endeavours to put forth with the help of it is of the abovementioned kind and hence it cannot be said to be tailored by dictates
of commensense or convention.   Rather, the only criterion that

needs to be taken into consideration is whether it is tenable. Condrakīrti further tells us that the view according to which states (of things) emerge through our expectations (of them) generated by causes (*hetu*) and experience (*pratyaya*) or by causes that we learn experiencially is sought to be disputed. For, we are told by the Buddha that *Bhāvas* not being caused at all that they are caused by one unitory cause or caused by non-homogeneous causes or caused by themselves or caused by other *Bhāvas* etc. are the different views that are sought to be disputed, and through their disputation a true nature of things that we normally experience is intended to be brought out. So long as we hold that things we normally experience emerge in this way we do not come to discover that emerging in this way is not their true nature. But so long as we do not intellectually and philosophically get out of this view there cannot come about its termination either.[30] Thus understood, *Pratītya Samutpāda* is a process of the emergence of our experience of things that we normally experience. While, as a theory, on the one hand, it amounts to explaining the way we normally hold things that we experience to be emerging, and on the other hand, through repudiation of the former theory as philosophically untenable it puts forth the view that *Bhāvas* do not emerge at all and hence they cannot be said to be *Pratītya Samutpānna* either.

Characteristics of Pratītya Samutpāda

When it is said that *Pratītya Samutpāda* has a number of characteristics and of them eight major characteristics are taken up by Nāgārjuna for detailed consideration in the opening stanza of the first chapter of his *Madhyamakaśāstra*, there being considerable disputation about them,[31] it needs to be understood as a process rather than a theory. According to Nāgārjuna there are eight prominent features of *Pratītya Samutpāda* which are as follows :[32] (1) *Anirodham*—*Pratītya Samutpāda* does not admit cessession. Candrakīrti tells us that cessession is denied first before denying emergence to bring to our notice that cessession necessarily does not presuppose prior emergence.[33] That is, there is no necessary connection between prior emergence and posterior cessession [34] We will be told that since there is no emergence of *Bhāvas*, there is no cessession of them either. This characteristic not only gives up cause-effect terminology but signifies non-causal *Santāna* or flow that is undisrupted. The coming and going of states is so smooth that it takes place without any obstruction. (ii) *Anutpādam*—Nāgārjuna holds that no one ever holds that *Bhāvas* have emerged out of themselves, of some other *Bhavas,* of both of them or even arbitrarily. (*ahetutaḥ*)[35] In fact Candrakīrti tells us that since they are self-existent i.e. come to be on their own to speak of their emergence is pointless.[36] Since Nāgārjuna not only repudiates *svabhāva* of *dharmas* but also holds that some items, free from dharmas, are self-existent,[37] they are real according to him even though ungenerated. But number of other items that come to be considered to be real are infact *Pratītya Samutpanna* and hence unreal. Such a process of their generation, again, is such that it has all along been with us. We are brought up and nurtured in the atmosphere of it. We simply do not know nor is there any way to tell since when such a process of generation ever began. Thus, *Pratītya Samutpāda* as a process, the way we normally consider things, properties, dispositions are generated is beginningless, but some items, in so far as they are there and are not generated at all, are ungenerated—i.e. beginningless. Though *Pratītya Samutpāda* as a theory has been long in circulation in the intellectual atmoshere and though no one generally knows who first came to offer that kind of explanation of the generation of the things, yet that in itself does not guarantee that the kind of explanation it gives is tenable. That is how those things which are not *Pratītya Samutpanna* will be anirodhita by the proper philosophical perspective, but those which are *Pratītya Samutpanna* will be nirodhita by such a perspective. But more of it in the fourth chapter. Meanwhile let us turn to the consideration of other features. (iii) *Anucchadam*—This feature of *Pratītya Samutpāda* has to be understood differently from the other feature of it viz. *Anirodham*. We said that *Pratītya Samutpāda* is a way of understanding emergence of items that we normally experience and take to be real. We come to understand that this mode of understanding the nature and emergence of things is untenable and hence to be discarded when and in so far as we come to develop a proper perspective. But even after we come to develop such a perspective the fact remains that others who do not come to develop such a perspective continue to hold that things and their very constitutive states are *Pratītya Samutpanna*. This being the case, there is every possibility that *Pratītya Samutpāda* will continue to have its impact on them. Thus understood, *Pratītya Samutpāda* cannot be got rid of totally such that no person is or shall come to be under its sway. That is why it is called *anuccheda*. (iv) *Aśāśvataṁ* —Though we normally regard things and their states, features and properties to be *Pratītya Samutpanna* and though normally we do not regard anything to be wrong and misleading in it, yet from this it does not follow that philosophical illumination shall not arise unless we consider them to be so. As we shall see, it precisely consists in understanding that to regard things that are *Pratītya Samutpanna* to be real is obstruction to it. In consequenc it is not inescapable, inevitable and required to be adopted come what may, and that is how it is *aśāśvata* as well. (v) *Anekārtham—Pratītya Samutpāda* as an expression has more than one semantical imports. In one sense it is a theory or doctrine brought forward to explain emergence of and change in things—i.e. to account for change and continuity as features of the world. Secondly, it is understood as a process in which things are said to be given to us as also a process through and because of which things are generated or they change etc. Thirdly, it is said to be making a certain world-view called *Saṁsāra* available to us and in this kind of world-view everything that is said to belong to the world comes to be considered to be endowed with certain features which on closer scrutiny turn out to be philosophically uninteresting and untenable. But in so far as *Pratītya Samutpāda* presents such a semantic complexity and variety it is said to be *anekārtha*. (vi) *Anānātham*—Though *Pratītya Samutpāda* presents this kind of plurality of its semantic import, yet, it by no means presents alternative world-perspectives such that one can find at least one of them to be philosophically interesting and tenable. Rather, in spite of such plurality of semantic import that it presents, it brings forth only a unitory world-view[38] in which everything that we experience, feel, conceive etc is not only considered to be real but also constituting part of the furniture of the same world. (vii) *Anāgamaṁ* — It is a fact that one comes to be brought up and nurtured into the atmosphere and framework of *Pratītya Samutpāda* right from one's childhood. There is no question, therefore, as to how is it that one comes to adopt *Pratītya Samutpāda* view of things and the corresponding world-view that it presents. But, it is indeed inscrutable and enigmatic as to why does one come to bring himself to accept such a view? On investigation it would be clear that one has not of choice and consciously brought oneself to accept such a world-view. In this sense relationship between *Pratītya Samutpāda* and any layman or even a person on whom proper philosophic illumination has not dawned is such that he does not accept such a theory because it is philosophically more satisfoctory. In fact one does not consciously and with full knowledge accept it. That is why, it is called *anāgamaṁ*. Lastly, (viii) *Anirgamaṁ*—Though one does not come to bring oneself to accept *Pratītya Samutpāda*, yet however unknowingly one may come to accept it, so long as proper perspective and requisite kind of philosophic illumination does not dawn upon one, one is simply unable to find one's exit from it, however intensely one may expect this to happen.

Purpose of Pratītya Samutpāda

Before we proceed to outline the theory of *Pratītya Samutpāda* as put forth by the Buddha[39] according to Nāgārjuna, and further explained by Candrakīrti, it would be instructive to inquire as to why the theory came to be put forth. We are told that the principal objective of *Pratītya Samutpāda* is to exhibit things and the world they inhabit as they are structured and constituted in order that we do not come to take a thing to be otherwise structured, in a way different from what it is.[40] The fundamental purpose behind *Pratītya Samutpāda* is to outline what is the case,[41] as a matter of fact regarding the world and things in it by trying to do away with otherwise misleading account of them that we are accustomed to give through errors and confusion.[42] Thus, it is the removal of normally and otherwise prevalent misunderstanding about the world and things in it that is the principal objective behind outlining the theory of *Pratītya Samutpāda*. For, unless and until misapprehension —no matter commonsensical or philosophic—is removed there is no hope of proper understanding being dawned on us. Doing away of misapprehension about the world and things in it is, thus, one aspect of the theory under consideration. It is to this end that much of Nāgārjuna's criticism of the then prevalent inrerpretations of *Pratītya Samutpāda* in particular and Buddha's philosophic position in general that is directed. But alongside of this is also the abovementioned another aspect of the programme—viz. to sketch out what according to him is the nature, structure and constitution of things and the world, they inhabit according to the Buddha. Since *Pratītya Samutpāda* occupies such a centrally located place in Buddha's philosophy, we are told, that to explicate and outline properly the theory of *Pratītya Samutpāda* is one of the principal aims of the *Madhyamakaśāstra* itself.[43] This is, further, quite natural. For, the principal concern of *Mādhyamikas*, like Nāgārjuna, is to outline the nature, structure and constitution of things and the world they inhabit[44] and since *Pratītya Samutpāda* is a theory specially designed to do so, it is but natural that they exploit it to the utmost possible extent.[45] Thus, in putting forth the theory of *Pratītya Samutpāda* Nāgārjuna in particular and *Mādhyamikas* in general have two inter connected aims : (a) on the positive side, the theory is aimed at outlining the nature, structure and constitution of things and the world they inhabit, as the Buddha wanted us to understand them and inquire whether and to what sort of change and/or continuity could be considered to be structural feature of them, and, (b) to expose critically the shortcomings in the accounts of them put forth by laymen or philosophers at the time – the philosophers of the Buddhist or non-Buddhist camp— with a view to tell us that either those accounts of things and the world they inhabit in terms of *Prakṛti, Iśvara, svabhāva, kāla, aṇus* etc. are wrought with difficulties,[46] in so far as they make some or the other agency responsible for change and emergence[47] or that such a nature of things and world as is imagined to be is often untenable, as the kind of things that are taken to be real are not so.[48] Thus understood, the purpose of *Pratītya Samutpāda* as a theory is very complex and one cannot be said to have given a satisfactory sketch of it as Nāgārjuna wanted it to be understood unless both these aspects of the theory are accounted for. The complexity of the theory is made further complicated by the fact that at the hands of Nāgārjuna both these aspects of the theory are very intimately connected. To be, therefore, in a position to deal with the theory and bring out its strong and weak points it is necessary to begin with a sketch of *Pratītya Samutpāda* as a general theory of emergence of and change in things that belong to the world.

General Account of Pratītya Samutpāda

For the kind of general account, again, it is not necessary to turn to any other work of Nāgārjuna or to a work of any other Buddhist writer for that matter. The entire 26th chapter of *Madhyamakaśāstra* is devoted to it. What it aims at presenting is an outline of the emergence of and change in things that are real and said to be belonging to the world. It is held that the items that emerge and are said to belong to the world are of two main kinds : external (*bāhya*) and internal (*ādhyātmika*). Now, understanding *Pratītya Samutpāda* to be a theory of emergence of and change in things, it will have two aspects : a) one, accounting for emergence of and change in external things and b) second one to account for those of internal things. Further, such an emergence of and change in things is sought to be accounted for in two principal ways : in terms of *Hetus* (*Hetūpani-bandhatah*) and in terms of *Pratyayas* (*Pratyayopani-bandhaśca*). No matter what kind of thing it is and however it is said to emerge, there are, it is held, twelve important links (*aṅga*) in the process of its emergence, which are said to be operative towards making such an emergence possible through clustering (*saṁghāta*) and creating impact upon one another. The twelve links are : A) misapprehension (*avidyā*), B) illicit impressions (*samskāra*), C) personal experiences (*vijñāna*), D) name (able)s and form (ed object)s (*nāmarūpa*), E) six organs (*ṣaḍāyatana*) F) contact (between organs and things) (*sparśa*), G) sensation (*vedanā*), H) desire (*tṛṣṇā*), I) substratum (*upādāna*), J) *abhāva*, K) birth or emergence (*jarā*) and L) degeneration, extinction leading to annoying states of affairs resulting into pain and displeasure. Of them the former in the link is said to generate the latter till the whole process is completed with regard to the given items.[49]

Emergence of external things is explained, on the above account thus : There are *Pudgalas* (material ultimates) of six main kinds, *Prthivi, Āp, Tejas, Vāyu, Ākāśa* and *Vijñana.*[50] They form into clusters called *Skandhas.* While all inanimate objects that belong to the world are made up of the clusters of first five *dhātus,* while in the case of human beings all the *dhātus* go to produce or generate them. The various states these things come to pass through, the various traits, properties they have are also explained to be emerging causatively and/or experientially.

The emergence of internal things is also said to proceed through the same kind of generative chain. It is on the basis of general pattern of the emergence of the things sketched above that our various feelings, sensations, emotions, etc. and consequent pleasure-pain etc. are said to emerge. This is said to be *hetūpanibandha* internal *Pratītya Samutpāda*. But *Pratītya Samutpāda* of internal things due to *pratyayas* is also explained similarly. It is held that inflexibility and rigidity of our body is due to *Pṛthividhātu*, while its blood flesh is said to be generated out of *Āpdhātu*. The food that we eat generates heat through its being digested and is held to be due to *Tejasdhātu*. The breathing is said to be ,caused by *Vāyudhātu*. While the end of body or death is due to *Ākāśadhātu*. *Manovijñāna* is said to be generated by *vijñānadhātu*. All these *dhātus* together are said to generate the whole person with its characteristic ego (*ahaṁ*). None of these *dhātus* singulaɪly could be said to be existence, life, animal, human being—man or woman. Nor is it said to belong to anybody.[51] The various kinds of items that so emerge are said to form an incessant flow like that of a river.[52]

On this count of the emergence of and change in things various kinds of items—external and internal, abstract and concrete, ontological and epistemological, cognitive and explanatory - are said to belong to the world with equal plausibility. Things that are there as a matter of fact as also those that are taken to be there—warrantably so or not—real as well as imaginary, experienced or noɩ are said to emerge and undergo change in the same way. All such items are said to create a similar impact on us and upon one another in the same way. Thus, the process of emergence of things goes on incessantly and uninterruptedly, the various items that emerge being just points or items in the flow or chain and yet none isolated, being dependent upon something else and connected with something other. The things, thus, form an interconnected link, a huge chain, an enormous flow from which nothing can get out.

The account of emergence outlined above has number of prominent characteristics : a) It is anthropocentric in the sense that it would be available only in a world where human beings and other items that belong to the world cohabit it and have generative impact upon one another. That is how emergence of things and beings, items that are external and internal, taking all of them to be on par with one another, comes to be explained in the same model. b) The nature, structure and constitution of things that it outlines is similar for all the items, whatever their status—ontological or othsrwise. c) It seeks to explain emergence of a later link in the chain on the proviso that earlier link is real and ontological without inquiring whether such a presupposition is tenable and if so what basis   d) If all these items are said to belong to the world with equal legitimacy and warrant then the world that comes before us remains too complicated to understand. This move reminds one of Aristotelian charge : to multiply number of items that belong to the world in order that we may come to understand better those which actually belong to it. Lastly, e) it presupposes that not only all these items belong to the world but also that they are causally related with one another. If one intends to present a philosophic account of the nature, structure and constitution of things that properly speaking belong to the world and outline some of the prominent errors and confusions we succumb to in explaining nature of things, then one has to take a very critical view of this kind of explanation of the world and things that are said to belong to it. One has, in fact, to formulate number of criteria, lay down various methodological principles, adopt certain methodological tools, cherish certain perspective. Only then will one be able to develop a certain philosophic position. It is this task that Nāgārjuna addresses himself to and that is the principal aim of his treatise—*Madhyamakaśāstra.*

As we shall see soon, this is not how Nāgārjuna intends to understand *Pratītya Samutpāda* and yet take it to be a theory of the nature and structure of things that properly belong to the world and of the world. Indeed, understanding *Pratītya Samutpāda* to be the theory of the emergence of *real things* and yet to be also a theory as to how the things that properly belong to the world are structured would be inconsistent. For, if anything that is *Pratītya Samutpanna* is to be taken to be real in the genuine sense of the term, it is very difficult to imagine what kind of things would come to be considered as non-genuine and hence not properly belonging to the world. In order that we come to describe that world alone that is inhabited by genuinely ontological things number of points will have to be paid a closer attention to : a) we must not come to consider genuinely ontological things to be otherwise than what they are, b) we must not consider those things which are not ontological to be ontological, and c) we must have at our disposal a well-defined criterion on the basis of which alone we are going to consider genuinely ontological things to be so.　To be able to get a clue to Nāgārjuna's views on these points let us probe into them little deeper.

Nāgārjuna on 'Tattva' and 'Tathya' :

In order to know what according to Nāgārjuna is real it would be instructive to ¦consider the meaning he gives to the two expressions viz. *'Tattva'* and *'Tathya'*.　According to him anything that is *Pratītya Samutpanna* is not generated naturally (svabhāvataḥ) and cannot be real in the genuine sense of the term.[53]　*Saṁvṛtti,* or what commonsensically and generally happens to be taken to be real because it is *Pratītya Samutpanna* is not genuinely real according to him.[54]　If anything ¦is real it cannot be got rid of, being genuinely existent and if anything is not there at all, then that, too, cannot likewise be got rid of, it just not being there.[55]　That nature of becoming (*bhāva*) that can be experienced but cannot be communicated (*aparapratyayam*) is *tattva.*[56]　Elsewhere he tells us that *tattva* is that which is incommunicable, undisturbed, incapable of being captured in language, free from *vikalpas* (concepts) and is unitory.[57] *Tathya* (genuine fact) is that which cannot be otherwise from it is.[58]　According to Nāgārjuna in particular and *Mādhyamikas* in general the world is constituted of clusters (*skandhas*) which are impermanent, some happen to be destroyed while others happen to be generated.　But it is not the case that those *skandhas* that happen to be destroyed themselves are regenerated. When those *skandhas* which are liable to be destroyed vanish, at that very time those which are liable to be generated emerge. Thus the world is constituted of such an incessant flow of items, which are either given in succession or simultaneously.　But none of them is permanent.[59]　The world genuinely speaking is made up *skandhas* that are constituted of peculiar states natu-rally such that neither the *skandhas* nor their states are *Apratītya-samutpanna.*[60]　The world as a whole is certainly not liable to be destroyed, nor is it produced or generated, the items that genuine-ly belong to it are, however, such that none of them is eternal. Rather it is short-lived and their being given in succession makes for a flow, or water-current of a river.　We shall return to some of these points later.　For the present it suffices for the purpose at hand.

Nāgārjuna's World-View

A closer look at some of the points will show that according to Nāgārjuna the mark of a genuinely real item is that it cannot be considered otherwise than what it is. Anything to which this criterion cannot be applied cannot be considered to be a genuinely ontological thing in his view. Candrakīrti, elaborating some of the implications of Nāgārjuna's view, argues that items that are so genuinely considered to be real are such that the nature of any one of them has nothing in common with the nature of any other.[61] Thus, the items are not only discrete but also that no two of them have anything in common. We shall return to this point little later. For the present it suffices to note that the things that are taken to be real, according to Nāgārjuna, are so taken on the ground that each one of them fulfils a certain criterion. The approach is, thus, philosophic, rather than commonsensical. It does not take what commonsensically is taken to be real as real. It has a well defined criterion and the criterion is sought to be applied consistently. Secondly, the notion of real so formulated can be said to be restrictive in the sense that it does exclude some items from being taken to be real—indeed many. But in so far as it does retain reality of some, while it excludes that of others it cannot be said to be too weak and inclusive for that matter. For, it by no means amounts to taking something that cannot even in principle be taken to be real as real. Lastly, those things which are considered to be genuinely ontological are not taken to be so arbitrarily, but rather on the ground of fulfilment of a criterion. There might well be an element of arbitrariness in the criterion that is adopted, but once it is adopted it is not sought to be applied arbitrarily. This kind of rigor and consistency are some of the chief tenets of Nāgārjuna's thought as we shall see in the present study.

Thus, on Nāgārjuna's view the world is not a dream, a fiction. It is not even an empty box as many times it is held to be. This view, as we shall argue in the next chapter, stems from a very serious kind of misunderstanding about one of the central pillars of his philosophic endeavour—viz. *Śūnyatā*. Restricting for the present to *Pratītya Samutpāda*, too, we find surprisingly, that the way various scholars have tried to make sense of it as Nāgārjuna understands it, is far too at variance from what he upholds. For example, it is held that *Pratītya Samutpāda* according to Nāgārjuna is a theory of the emergence of various kinds of things that are said to belong to the world. We saw that such is not the case. He does not wish to understand *Pratītya Samutpāda* that way. His problem rather is to present that kind of account of the world and things that genuinely belong to it which will expose some of the major pitfalls and errors of the way in which things are said to be emerging in the world generally and commonsensically. This kind of critical examination of the generally held view of emergence and cessation of things goes on throughout the entire text. This is not something which is peculiar to Nāgārjuna. This characteristic feature is also noticeable in the way the Buddha is said to have philosophised and Nāgārjuna merely follows him in his footsteps.[62] Thus, instead of outlining his theory of the nature of the world alone he comes to do that through a detailed critical examination of the theory that is normally and commonsensically accepted and elaborated, with a view to bring home to us the misunderstandings, errors and confusions it is beset with. On this background he outlines—here and there—that kind of theory or account of the world and things belonging to it which will bring out what the Buddha had to say on the point. It is to put forth such a novel theory that is his principal aim. Rather, to remove misunderstandings about Buddha's theory is his fundamental objective and positively to outline that view of the world as the Buddha intended to put forward. That is why in the *Vigrahavyāvartani* he proclaims : if there are any defects in the theory presented then they are not mine; since I do not wish to put forth any of my theory, I cannot be held responsible for any defects in the theory that is outlined.[63] Be that as it may.

Nāgārjuna on 'Svabhāva'

At the hands of Nāgārjuna, in his attempt to outline the nature of things that are genuinely real and that properly belong to the world, the notion of *Svabhāva* (true nature) plays an important role. *Svabhāva* is considered to be so crucially important because a genuinely real thing alone is said to have such a feature that marks it off from everything that is not so real. In other words, *svabhāva* is a differentia of genuinely real things.

Svabhāva is such a nature or feature of a thing that never for-
sakes it i.e. there can be no genuinely real thing without its own
feature.[64] It is further argued that such a feature of a genuine
thing that marks it off from others is such that it is inconceivable to hold regarding it that it is *Pratītya Samutpanna i.e.* to have
emerged out of *Pratyayas* or *Hetus* or both.[65] Thus, while in
the case of things that are *Pratītyasamutpanna* not only they but
even their nature and features too, are *Pratītya Samutpanna*, in
the case of those genuinely real things that are not *Pratītyasamutpanna* have a differentiating feature that their characteristic
feature is also not *Pratītyasamutpanna*. Such a *svabhāva* of a
thing is said to be non-spurious[66] as also non-artificial[67] and
ungenerated. It is not only told that *svabhāva* not only cannot
be different from what it is[68] but also that any *svabhava* that is
Pratītyasamutpanna is spuriously so.[69] Thus understood, *svabhāva*
is crucially important feature of a genuinely real thing. It not
only marks it off from anything that is *Pratītyasamutpanna* for
the simple reason that none of them can have such a feature,
but also from other genuinely real things, because *svabhava* of
no two real things will have anything in common. Every
genuinely real thing is a unit set as it were, such that none of
its feature is also a feature of some other similarly structured
set. Discretness of genuinely real things is thus made possible by
their characteristic *svabhāva*.

Crucial Tenets of Nāgārjuna's Account of the World

We remarked earlier that at the hands of Nāgārjuna *Pratītya
Samutpāda* does not remain a blanket and inclusive theory of the
emergence or generation of all those things that are said to
belong to the world, their features, states, interconnections,
mutual impact—all of these understood ordinarily and sought to
be explained commonsensically. Instead, it becomes a theory
within the framework of which those and only those things are
said to inhabit the world which are genuinely real, none of which
is *Pratītyasamutpanna*, or none of the characteristic and unique
feature of which is also said to be *Pratītyasamutpanna*. Such
an ontological world is indeed sparely populated in so far as
everything that is commonsensically taken to be real and constitutive of the world is not so taken. But such an account of the
world differs from the commonsensical account of it in other

major respects also. Some of those are : (1) on commonsensical account of the nature, structure and constitution of the world things of far too different kinds are said to inhabit and constitute the world and thereby make the world so thickly populated that it becomes well nigh impossible to decide which of them are genuinely ontological and which are not so. It also paves a way for an unsurmountable kind of platonism, which as a philosophical theory of the world has quite a number of unpallatable consequences. Nāgārjuna's account, on the contrary, paves a way for nominalism in so far as only one kind of things—genuinely ontological—alone are said to belong to the world. This is decided, further, not arbitrarily but on the basis of a well-formulated criterion, as remarked earlier. (2) On commonsensical view things no doubt change and thus change is a feature of the world—structurally and constitutionally. For, things that belong to the world themselves change. But they change under the pressure exerted on them by other things. Every change is, on this view, caused by or affected from some other things, since, though things have perhaps dispositions to change, yet change does not occur in an isolated thing. Sometimes such a change is effected by priorily existing thing and often change is sought to be accounted for on the basis of the fact that the thing that is said to cause change and the thing that changes are given to us in succession. It is held on the commonsensical view that every change is a causal change and any account of change that is non-causal is held to be unsatisfactory. Further, the dividing line between that which is posterior in sequence and that which is consequence is very thin and as a result the two are often mixed up—often the latter is mistaken for the former. On the count of continuity as a feature of the world it is held that same things at least—external or internal—are continuous and non-discrete. Indeed, some things are held to be eternal, no matter whether they change or not. Thus, on the non-Nagarjunian theory of *Pratītya Samutpāda*—a commonsical account of the emergence of the things and their features—things that constitute the world are not only mutually interconnected but also that they are causally connected. Against this account of change and continuity, causal explanation of things' interconnectedness etc. Nāgārjuna has number of reservations to voice. i) First, continuity as a feature of the world need not necessarily be based on eternality of at least some things that belong to it. World as a totality of things does not depend upon any particular thing. Nor does continuity as its feature need to be anchored in eternality of some of the things belonging to it. For, even though none of the things belonging to the world is eternal the world can be continuous in so far as some things that belong to the world at one time and at another time overlap and through such spiral overlapping of things belonging to the world at various times continuity as a feature of the world is quite satisfactorily accountable. Thus considered, continuity need not be considered to be a structural feature of the world. It could very will be functional or accidental. (ii) Secondly, on what grounds do we say some thing to be caused by another or one feature of a thing caused by another feature of it or of some other thing? Is it because, where A is considered to be the cause of B, A is necessary and/or sufficiet condition of the emergence of B? If so, on what warrantable grounds do we say so? If the fact that things are given successively is our basis of saying that they are causally connected then where is the requisite necessary connection between them? May it not, instead, be the case that their being given to us so successively is an accidental feature of them? On what reliable ground do we consider something to be consequence of something else? Mere succession? What happens when things are given simultaneously, especially when a cluster of them happens to be presented? Are we to hold here also that such clustered things are causally related? Through succession and simultaneous presentation things belonging to the world can at the most be said to be connected, but not necessarily causally. Further, priority-posteriority in presentation of things in succession is essentially a temporal notion and this kind of temporal feature of a thing cannot be said to be making it emerge or cause it to emerge. *Pratītya Samutpāda* as a theory of the world, at the hands of Nāgārjuna, brings out connectedness of things belonging to the world, but not causal connectedness. Lastly, if things belonging to the world are not only discrete but also such that no two of them have any shareable features then under such circumstances one thing cannot be said to be causing an other. For, causal connectedness demands that between cause and effect there is some shareability—however thin it might be. Hence, every change need not be taken to be causal one, though every causal change is a species of change. (iii) Thirdly, on commonsensical view, in our account of causal relatedness of things and their mutually causing one another we rely upon our sensation, feelings, emotions, expectations and many more things as determining such a causal connectedness of them. Nāgārjuna has number of reservations on this count and quite rightly. First, connections sought to be established on account of *Hetus* and *Pratyayas* cannot simply be presumed to be there. Even if such connections obtain we need to be sure that they are genuinely causal. Connections of the kind under consideration need to be examined, before acceptance, on the count of their tenability, reliability and acceptability. Secondly, we need to bear in mind that very often such connections arise out of the fact that we use certain kind of language, exploit a certain family of concepts and concentrate upon certain kind of illustrations without inquiring whether there are counter instances. To circumvent them a deeper inquiry is in order and the way is not to ignore them. Thirdly, very often than not those things which are said to be causally connected with one another and generative of one another on account of *Hetus* and *Pratyayas* are such that on closer scrutiny, they turn out to be not genuinely ontological. We cannot hope to illicitely smuggle non-genuinely or spuriously ontological things into the world. Through such devices we come to structure the world in such a way and make it inhabited by such items that are anchored in misnomers, errors, confusions, intellectual bewitchments and linguistic as well as conceptual traps. It is this consequence that is designed to be avoided — not arbitrarily but on the basis of a philosophical scrutiny into and cross-examination of the commonsensical account of the world.

A Leap Towards Śūnyatā

The sort of the account of the world that Nāgārjuna embarks upon giving of the world that is genuinely ontological and is inhabited by ontologically real things has to be understood properly. It is not a plan to set up another world over and above the world that is commonsensically believed to be there. Nor is it expected to construct *ab novo* those things that are said to belong to it. Far from it. Instead, the world that is generally taken to be there—the world that we inhabit—and the things that inhabit it along with us, the usual account of them, commonly accepted interconnections between or among them are expected to be scrutinized in such a way that those and only those things or items can be said to belong to it which on a philosophically satisfactory basis could be said to be genuinely ontological—however such an account of the world differs from its commonsensical account. Likewise, its differences from other possible philosophical accounts of such a world, too, should be immaterial, provided the intended account is tenable. Thus, what is expected to be done is to tailor off such a world from the commonsensically accepted one alongwith genuinely ontological items belonging to it. To be able to accomplish such a formidable job, we will need such a powerful methodological weapon which will be helpful in our endeavour of tailoring off a genuinely ontological world unarbitrarily and uncompromisingly. Further, such a tool or weapon has to figure well on the count of its philosophical respectability. Being armed with such a weapon alone can we hope to accomplish our task. The weapon, again, has to be wielded properly. For, otherwise the whole programme is likely to lead to consequences that are philosophically disastrous and intellectually unrewarding. The weapon has to be used and exploited, therefore, within the framework of intuitive and methodological constraints. Such a weapon under consideration is *Śūnyatā*. It is using this weapon that Nāgārjuna has accomplished his task of presenting a philosophically satisfactory account of the nature, structure and constitution of the world that is ontological and of the things inhabiting it. Our study of Nāgārjuna's account of the world cannot be said to have reached a respectable level without considering the methodological weapon, the way Nāgārjuna wields it and the methodological and intuitive constraints withinin the framework of which he wields it. For, without *Śūnyatā* as a methodological weapon Nāgārjuna's exercise would have been frought with arbitrariness. But such a kind of consequence has not emerged, as we shall see. It is to the task of the consideration of the nature of *Śūnyatā*, a powerful methodological tool at the hands of Nāgārjuna, that we turn in the next chapter.

NOTES

1. *Prasannapadā*; ......yāvadācāryanāgārjunasya viditāviparīta-prajñāpāramitānīteḥ. Upodghāta. p. 1.

2. *Ibid*, ...ata evedaṁ madhyamakaśāstraṁ praṇītamācāryeṇa neyanītārthasūtrāntavibhāgopadarśanārthaṁ/ p. 13.

3. *Ibid*, Katame sūtrāntā neyārthāḥ katame nītārthāḥ? ye sūtrāntā mārgāvatārāya nirdiṣṭāḥ...ta ucyante nītārthāḥ/ p. 14.

4. *Ibid*, Tatra ya ete....avidyātimiropahatamatinayanajñāna-viṣayāpekṣayā/p. 13.

5. *Ibid*, Tasmādutpādādideśanāṁ mṛṣārthāṁ...ārabdhavānācār-yaḥ/p. 14.

6. *Ibid*, Yasyaivaṁ...ācāryo yuktyāgamābhyāṁ saṁśayamith-yājñānāpākaraṇārthaṁ śāstramidamārabdhavān/p. 13.

7. Panday, G.C., *Studies in the origins of Buddhism*, p. 427 also Poussin, La D.V., *Philosophy (Buddhist)*, ERE, Vol. IX, p. 848.

8. Kalupahana. *Buddhist Philosophy—Historical Approach*, p. 29.

9. Davids, (Mrs.) Rhys, *Paticca Samutpāda*, ERE Vol. IX, p. 672.

10. Davids. (Mrs.) Rhys; *Buddhism*, p. 89.
 Cf. Hiriyanna, M. *Outline of Indian Philosophy*, p. 143.

11. Stcherbatsky, Th., *Buddhist Logic*, Vol. I, p. 116.

12. *Ibid*, p. 119.

13. Asmin sati idaṁ bhavati/Tattatprāpya yadutpannaṁ notpan-naṁ tat svabhāvataḥ/Nirvyāpāraḥ sarve dharmaḥ.

14. Stcherbatsky, Th., *The Conception of Buddhist Nirvāṇa* p. 94 and also frequent references. On page 192, the author thus remarks that "......comment upon Relativity, the work of the venerable master Candrakīrti."

15. Murti, T.R.V., *Central Philosophy of Buddhism*, p. 7.

16. Radhakrîshnan. S., *History of Philosophy* (Eastern and Western), p. 185.
 Also *Indian Philosophy*, Vol. I, pp. 646, 698.

17 Hume, D., *Treatise of Human Nature*.

18. Barlingay, S.S., *The Significance of Pratītya Samutpāda Sāmānyalakṣaṇa and Apoha in Buddhism* (Buddha Jayanti Lecture), p. 8.
     (Indian Philosophical Congress, XLV Session, December, 1971, Osmania University, Hyderabad).

19. *Prasannapadā*; Pratītyaśabdo'tra lyabantaḥ prāptāvapekṣāyaṁ vartate/p. 2.

20. *Ibid*, Samutpūrvaḥ...vartate/p. 2.

21. It is held, on the authority of *Abhidharmakoṣavyākhyā* that the view under consideration is that of Bhananta Śrīlābha. Cf. Vaidya, P.L. (ed.) *Madhyamakaśāstra*, p. 312.

22. *Prasannapadā*; Apare tu bruvate...nipātaḥ syāt/p. 2.

23. *Ibid*, Na ca etadevaṁ/...vyutpattirabhyupeyā/p. 2.

24. *Ibid*, Yastu "vīpsārthatvātpratyupasargasya,...ityanye/p. 3.

25. *Ibid*, Tena idānīṁ prāpya sambhavaḥ...na vīpsāyāḥ sambhandha iti/p. 3.

26. *Ibid*, Etadvā ayuktaṁ ...apekṣyaśabdaparyāyatvāt/p. 3.

27. *Ibid*, Prāptyarthasyaiva...ityabhyupagamāt/p. 3.

28. *Ibid*, Yaccāpi svamataṁ...vivakṣitatvāt/p. 3.

29. *Ibid*, Athāpi...nopapannaṁ/p. 3.

30. *Ibid*, Tadevaṁ hetupratyayāpekṣaṁ...nirgamo vidyate/p. 4.

31. *Ibid*, Anantaviśeṣaṇasambhave' pi...vivādāṅgabhūtatvāt/p. 4.

32. *Madhyamakaśāstra*, 1.1
     Anirodhamanutpādamanucchedamaśāśvataṁ/
     Anekārthamanānārthamanāgamamanirgamam//

33. *Prasannapadā*; Atra ca nirodhasya pūrvaṁ pratiṣedhaḥ......dyotayitum/p. 4.

34. *Ibid*, Tasmānnāyaṁ niyamo...nirodheneti/p. 4.

35. *Madhyamakaśāstra* 1.3
     Na svato nāpi parato na dvābhyāṁ nāpyahetutaḥ/
     Utpannā jātu vidyante bhāvāḥ kvacana kecana//

36. *Prasannapadā*; Na svata Utp,adyante...vaiyarthyāt/p. 7.

37. *Vigrahavyāvārtani—Svopajñavṛtti*; Na hi vayaṁ dharmāṇāṁ svabhāvaṁ...svabhāvamabhyupagacchāmaḥ/p. 292.

38. *Prasannapadā*; Nānārtho asya iti nānārtham bhinnārtham, Nanānārthaḥ anānārthaḥ abhinnārthamityarthaḥ/18.9 p. 159.

39. *Vigrahavyāvartani*; 72
Yaḥ Śūnyatāṁ Pratītyasamutpādaṁ Madhyamāṁ Pratipadamanekārthām
Nijagāda praṇamāmi tamapratimasambuddhaṁ/p. 295.

40. *Prasannapadā*; Partītya Samutpādasya...anyathā abhiniviśate/ p, 249.

41. *Ibid*. Evaṁ pratītya samutpādabhāvanayā tattvamavatarati/ p. 244.

42. *Ibid, Pratītyasamutpādasya*...avidyā prahīyate/p. 244.

43. *Prasannapadā*: Pratityasamutpādaḥ śāstrābhidheyārthaḥ/p. 2.

44. *Ibid*, Yathāvadviditavastusvarūpāṇāṁ mādhyamikānāṁ/ p. 187.

45. *Ibid*, Pratītyasamutpādavādino hi mādhyamikāḥ,...pratipannāḥ/pp. 156-57.

46. *Ibid*, ...prakṛtīsvarasvabhāvakālāṇu.../p. 65.

47. *Ibid*,kartṛvādanirāsena...p. 65.

48. *Ibid*, paraparikalpitaṁ satvaṁ asya nirākurmaḥ/p. 169.

49. *Ibid*, p. 245.

50. *Ibid*, Tatra saddhātavaḥ uktāḥ... p. 51.

51. *Ibid*, pp. 245-246.

52. *Ibid*. ......nadīsrotavat/p. 247.

53. *Ibid*, ācāryānāgārjuneva... iti abhyupagamāt/p. 3

54. *Ibid*. Saṁvṛttiḥ eva na tatvaṁ/p. 18.

55. *Ibid*, Tatra sanna nirvartate......assannapi avidyamānatvāt/ p. 28.

56. *Ibid*, aparapratyayaṁ bhāvānāṁ yat svarūpam tat tatvaṁ/ p. 159.

57. *Madhyamakaśāstra* 18.9
Aparapratyayaṁ śāntaṁ prapañcairapañcitaṁ/
Nirvikalpamanāanārthametattatvasy lakṣaṇaṁ//

58. *Prasonnapadā*, Tatra tathyaṁ nāma yasya...nāsti/p. 158.

59 *Ibid*, yasmādanye māraṇāntikāḥ...na śāśvatataḥ/p. 248.

60. *Ibid*, vicitrābhih avasthābhiḥ………svabhāvaṣūnyavādināṁ/ p. 224.

61. *Ibid*, Iha bhāvānāṁ anya asādhāraṇaṁ ātmīyaṁ yatsvarūpaṁ tat svalakṣaṇaṁ/p. 20.

62. *Prasannapadā*; Na Khalu āryāḥ lokavyahāreṇa upapattiṁ varnayanti,……tayā eva lokaṁ bodhayati/p. 19.

63. *Vigrahavyāvartani*, 29.

64. *Prasannapadā*; yaḥ dharmaḥ yaṁ padārthaṁ……svabhāvaḥ/ p. 105.

65. *Madhyamokaśāstra*, 15 1
Na sambhavaḥ svabhāvasya yuktaḥ pratyayahetubhiḥ/

66. *Prasannapadā*; yaḥ akṛtakaḥ sa svabhāvaḥ/p. 114.

67. *Ibid*, akṛtrimasvabhāvasya sarvathā anutpāda……p. 116.

68. *Ibid*, Svabhāvasya anyathātvaṁ nāsti/p. 222.

69. *Ibid*, Hetuyratyayasambhūtaḥ svabhāvaḥ kṛtakaḥ/

CHAPTER III

ŚŪNYATĀ

In the preceeding chapter it has been pointed out that Nāgārjuna employs the methodological tool called *Śūnyatā* to accomplish the task of tailoring off the genuinely real world from that which is accepted as real on commonsensical ground. It is to seeing how Nāgārjuna exploits such a powerful weapon that this chapter is aimed at. Any tool when it is employed to carry out a certain job must come to function within certain methodological and intuitive constraints, within the framework of which it can be exploited. Otherwise, there is every possibility of its misuse resulting into unpallatable and disastrous consequences. As a tool it must again have to be amenable to use in any domain of knowledge without special reference to any specific sphere and as such when it is utilized it will have only certain kind of consequences to give rise to. One more thing about such a tool is that it must be neutral in its applicability. That is, its being wielded need not necessarily be tied down to subscription to a particular philosophical position. It is needless to say that *Śūnyatā* as a methodological tool at the hands of Nāgārjuna also has these features. Nāgārjuna wields such a refined and sharpened tool to get a clear insight into the problems before him. So in this chapter we propose to outline : (i) the way Nāgārjuna exploits *Śūnyatā* as a methodological tool to clear up the otherwise thick fog of philosophical misinterpretation and confusion and to account for those and only those items which are genuinely real. (ii) the bearings of *Śūnyatā* as a tool on certain philosophical problems falling within the sphere of ontology, epistemology, logic etc and (iii) to give a sketch of the connection of *Śūnyatā* with *Pratītyasamutpāda*—a theory about the nature of the world alongwith the genuinely real things inhabiting it on the one hand and also its connection with *Nirvaṇā*—a proper perspective that one needs to develop in order that one comes to adopt such a philosophical position as the Buddha wants us to adopt on the other. This is, again, not because they are considered to be pillars of Nāgārjuna's philosophy but especially for the reason that at the hands of Nāgārjuna, who commences his treatise—*Madhyamakaśāstra*—with exposition of *Pratītya Samutpāda,* the three—viz. *Pratītya Samutpāda, Śūnyatā* and *Nirvāṇa*—are so intimately connected that none of them could be understood in isolation from the other two. But more importantly, we are also told by Nāgārjuna that rightly understood *Pratītya Samutpāda* and *Śūnyatā* converge upon the same philosophical position called *Madhyamā Pratipad.*[1] This of course turns out to be the case through the prism of proper perspective called—*Nirvāna* cannot be overlooked. For, without it, the development of a proper perspective will be thwarted and in the absence of such a perspective one's coming to subscribe to a philosophical position that the Buddha intended, according to Nagarjuna, to uphold would also remain a far removed possibility. Having considered, therefore, the import of *Pratītya Samutpāda* we turn to *Śūnyatā*, a methodological tool at Nāgārjuna's hand.

Methodological and Intuitive Constraints :

Any tool worth the name can be said to be operative not without any constraints whatever. Such constraints are generally of two principal kinds : methodological as well as intuitive. *Śūnyatā* as a tool is not an exception to it. Such constraints need to be understood before hand in order that we neither come to utilize the tool in whichever indiscrete way we are pleased to, so as to avoid its exploitation giving rise to consequences that are sought to be avoided. It, therefore, will not merely do to say that *Śūnyatā* is a methodological tool. It has to be specified the constraints within which it is expected and designed to be wielded. Of them, the intutive constraints will enable us to comprehend those considerations about it which we do not wish to sacrifice in so far as they are intuitively indubitable and hence certifiable. Even in philosophy where methodological tools like *Śūnyatā* come to be exploited with the purpose of getting a better and clearer insight into certain issues, the insight that we shall come to gain cannot compel us to sacrifice that which is intuitively indubitable. On the count of methodological constraint, likewise, there surface certain restrictions. A given tool has to be wielded in a certain way, exploited for certain purposes, and utilized with certain restrictions. Overlooking such methodological constraints is not only disastrous elsewhere but also in philosophy. For example, though it is true that the Buddha did not commit himself to any specific metaphysical view yet this in itself does not establish that he had nothing to say, whatever, that could be considered as metaphysically significant. This needs to be made sense of with extreme caution and with the help of such a methodological weapon which will enable us to make sense of his unwillingness to discuss certain metaphysical issues at all. But on the other hand, the tool under consideration would be such that it should not empty his philosophy of any and every metaphysical issue just because it is a metaphysical issue and nothing else. Or broadly still, from the fact that the Buddha did not consider certain issues to be philosophically interesting and illuminating, one should not jump to the conclusions that no philosophical issue, according to the Buddha, was worth discussing and entertaining. If such a conclusion comes to be derived on the basis of exploitation of a methodological tool that comes to be wielded outside of its warranted sphere—the sphere which alone it is expected to be profitably exploited and with utter disregard to the methodological constraints, then, too, we would be giving such an outline of Buddha's philosophical position that is at variance from the one that he could be said to be entertaining. Our coming to disregard or distort at least those ontological and/or epistemological issues which a philosopher did pay serious attention to cannot be the basis for our saying that the kind of philosophical position that turns out to be an outcome of such consideration is in fact the one that he wanted to uphold and defend. One's criticising the views held by a certain philosopher on a justifiable basis is one thing, but to end up with such a sketch of someone's philosophical position that is essentially different from the one he intended to champion and that, too, on the basis of illicit exploitation of a methodological tool, is quite another. Many of the misunderstandings about Buddha's philosophy, according to Nāgārjuna, arose, unfortunately, out of disregard for methodological constraints on *Śūnyatā*.

This kind of trouble arises with a tool—even a methodological one—especially because it does not become available only to its legitimate utilization such that in the context of its unwarranted exploitation it simply ceases to be operative. The kind of neutrality of a tool makes it vulnerable to be exploited in a manner one is pleased to. For instance, a surgical knife may be used to perform an operation or to stab somebody. But the latter kind of exploitation of it is something that falls outside the methodological constraint within which it is expected to be used. Disregarding such constraint about a philosophically significant tool in philosophy does not pave way for philosophical illumination. Rather it hinders that kind of philosophical illuminasion which otherwise is likely to arise. As we shall see, Nāgārjuna quite often voices his opposition to such kind of disregard to methodological constraints with which *Śūnyatā* is intended to be used. His opposition of this kind is not, therefore, to be understood, as the opposition for the sake of it but rather as the one that originates in the methodological constraints of *Śūnyatā*. Considered thus, it is defensible and it is also reasonable that he complains about scholars disregarding such methodological constraints about *Śūnyatā* and in turn giving rise to what could at the best be called caricatures of Buddha's philosophy or at least caricatures of Nāgārjuna's philosophic understanding of Buddha's teaching.

The other constraint, viz. intuitive, concerning *Śūnyatā* arises not so much out of its being a tool, that it comes to be put to an illicit use of it, but rather out of its very nomenclature. It needs, however, to be understood that it is a technical expression and needs to be understood in its technical sense. If, instead of this, we take it to be an expression on par with any other expression that is understood literally and even when it is so understood does not create any semantic or philosophical problem, then, however proximate we might be to the intuitive dictates, we thereby come to embrace such consequences which are philosophically disastrous. Here we disregard its technical sense and instead come to be carried away by the literal sense of the expression '*Śūnyatā*' that is intuitively apparent. Once it is understood that it is a technical expression and not a non-technical one intuitive constraint demends that it is not to be understood commonsensically and literally. If understood in the latter sense, it will lose its technical sense and in that case it will come to be operative, as a methodological tool, in such context that are at variance from the intended one. As we shall see, one of the major mistakes of Nagarjuna's *Pūrvapakṣin* consists in disregarding this kind of intuitive constraint on *Śūnyatā* and thereby misunderstandingly interpreting *Śūnyatā* as an expression openly literally. This is how, according to him (Nāgārjuna's *Pūrvapakṣin*) acceptance of *Śūnyatā* makes nonsense of everything—*Pratītya Śamutpāda, Nirvāṇa* and even of four noble truths (*āryasatyas*). For, understood literally, *Śūnyatā*, according to him, means *abhāva* in its various senses—non-obtainability, untenability, unacceptability etc. We shall have occasion to consider Nāgārjuna's protest against this kind of misunderstanding *Śūnyatā*. For the present, however, it suffices to note that it needs to be understood within the framework of the two above mentioned major kinds of constraints—methodological and intuitive.

Nāgārjuna, having an insight into the problems and issues, could see that the Buddha has used *Śūnyatā* as a weapon, explained it at a greater length, and exploited it to cut off much of the ontological and epistemological rubbish with which what is genuinely there comes to be polluted. Having developed a proper insight into the use of *Śūnyatā* and being fully aware of its intuitive and methodologicol constraints, he could put forth a philosophically satisfactory account of the nature, structure and constitution of the world and the only real inhabitants of it. He was immensely helped in his endeavour of presenting such an account of the world through the judicious and philosophically interesting utilization of this powerful weapon. So, without further delay, we turn to give an account of Nāgārjuna's treatment of *Śūnyatā* and draw attention to some of the crucially significant consequences of it.

Śūnydtā : A Jans-Faced Notion

Śūnyatā, as a methodological tool at the hands of Nāgārjuna, is operative in two important ways and accordingly it has two significant facets of it. On the first count, it functions as preservative of that world-view and that world which a legitimate understanding of *Pratītya-Samutpāda* as outlined in the previous chapter, is supposed to make available to us. On the second count, on the contrary, it functions as destructive of that world-view and that world which commonsensical understanding

of *Pratītyasamutpāda* outlined in the previous chapter is supposed to bring forth. By and large, scholars come to concentrate
almost exclusively on the latter aspect of it and subscribing to
its literal interpretation come to champion a view according to
which nothing afterall is real and tenable according to Nāgārjuna
and hence Nāgārjuna seeks to preach, it is held, the philosophy
of void or nothingness. Nothing, as we shall see, could be
further from truth. These two aspects of *Śūnyatā* are to be
simultaneously operative in Nāgārjuna's philosophical investigations, though they are operative in the two above-mentioned
distinct senses.

The entire consideration of *Śūnyatā* as a methodological
tool, in its second aspect, as we understand it, falls into three
main spheres. In its ontological perspective, the notion appears
to mean that what is given in this world are merely particular
things, that they are so particular and separate that no two of
them are either similar or identical. Each one of them is uniquely particular and having the same status as the others have.
None of them is eternal and everlasting nor are they so evanes-
cent as we are taught them to believe. Thus, ontologically
speaking, it amounts to nothing else but the advocacy and acceptance of uniquely particular and discrete things as part and
parcel of the furniture of the world. They are connected only
in so far as they are given to us either in succession or simultaneously. But for that matter they cannot be said to be causally
connected.

According to the epistemological perspective the advocacy
of the notion of *Śūnyatā* boils down to the acceptance that there
are certain knowledge claims which are such that they can be
certifiable as well as warrantable. It further tells us that our
knowledge is always of extreme particular thing. On this level
the notion rejects the contention that human knowledge is an
empty set or that 'nothing is knowable'. It only advocates that
on the basis of our knowledge of one porticular thing we shall
never be in a position to comprehend the nature of any other
particular thing. Thus, given a, b, c, d or e as discrete particular
things what sort of knowledge can one claim, at the best, to be
at one's disposal? Naturally one will have the knowledge of 'a'
separately, 'b' separately, 'c' separately and so on. It is irrele-
vant whether such things are given simultaneously or in succession. This in itself should not make any fundamental change

to our knowledge of them. That sometimes they are given in succession amounts to saying that our knowledge of such thing comes in succession. Or else, what we might know is their succession. Yet, it cannot be maintained on this basis, that there is involved an element of causal connection or dependency in such kind of succession. Though it may be a matter of fact that "a state of 'a' being known" might precede "a state of 'b' being known" or though 'a' occur prior to 'b' or both 'a' and 'b' might be given to us simultaneously, and although it is legitimate to say that the two states or two things are connected with one another, yet, just on this ground, in any case, one cannot invent a causal connection among these things as it is commensensically held to be the case. Therefore, we cannot hope to maintain that there is a causal connection between or among these states. Nor can we hold things to be causally related. 'It means that our knowledges of particular things do not either fully or partially or even spirally overlap. Our discovery of each one of the particular thing is a fresh endeavour that neither presupposes any such efforts nor does it arise as a consequence of our prior discovery of any particular thing. Thus, on the epistemological level an employment of the notion of *Śūnyatā* as a methodological tool holds that our knowledge of different discrete genuine entities, too, is discrete'[2], and thereby rejects the nihilistic interpretations that 'nothing is knowable' as well as realistic interpretation that the knowledge of everything that we experience, perceive, imagine is certifiable no matter whether it is genuinely real so or not.

Although these two aspects of *Śūnyatā* are important they are not the only aspects of it. There is a third aspect and perhaps equally important one and it is that the notion is applicable on logico-linguistic plane. According to this perspective, granted that we employ certain words, symbols, expressions for description of certain objects, there arise certain questions (1) What is it that compels us to employ such expressions? (2) Is the knowledge which we acquire through such descriptions certifiable? (3) If so, what is it that sanctions such an employment of a descriptive language? Not only that, but how are we going to show that the method adopted in the description of the things is warrantable? That means, if the things in the world are bare particulars and if the knowledge of such bare particular things, too, is particular, then, can we properly envisage any methodological device which not only fulfils our expectations but at the same time also succeeds in grouping certain things under one head without disturbing each one of the members of that group of objects either structurally and/or functionally? These questions Nāgārjuna appears to give utmost important to, when he is dealing with the notion of *Śūnyatā*, where the notion functions, according to him, in three different ways : (1) censor of *dharma* (predicate and predicative language) (2) censor of P*adārtha* (conceptual and categorical frame), and (3) censor of *nihsvabhāva bhāva* (*nihsvabhāva* states and modalities)[3]. These three functions of the notion of *Śūnyatā*, as we understand it, are termed as *Sarvadharma Śūnyatā*,[4] *sarvapadārtha śūnyatā*[5] and *nihsvabhāva bhāva śūnyata*,[6] respectively. All these three aspects of the notion of *śūnyatā* on logico-linguistic level are interpreted as having utmost importance, as it deals with the intellectual surgical operation leading to the advocacy of nominalistic approach to the philosophy of the Buddha as explained at the hands of Nāgārjnna. Alongwith them we also see one more use of *Śūnyatā* as a methodological tool which in Nāgārjuna's deliberations assumes considerable importance. It is known as censor of *dṛṣtis* (opinion)—*Sarvadṛṣtiśūnyatā*,[7] which is directed towards the nullification of all unwarrantable viewings. Studying the notion of *Śūnyatā* in this way, seems to us not only novel in its attempt but also appears to be throughly inconsistent with the traditional interpretation of it. Such an attempt of studying the notion of *Śūnyatā* will considerably pave a ground to examine critically whether and to what extent the efforts made under the banner of Copernican revolution[8] or the efforts made for the restoration of traditional interpretation of the notion of *Śūnyatā* as nihilism are genuine,[9] justifiable as well as warrantable. But in order to prepare an adequate ground for such a scrutiny, let us probe into the problem little deeper.

Śūnyatā : An ontological Aspect

It appears that behind the advocacy of the view that the official position of *Mādhyamikas* or of Nāgārjuna is nihilism, there are two prominent reasons. One is that scholars appear to have wrongly interpreted the notion of *Śūnyatā* in the sense of emptiness. They might have perhaps been led to put forth such a view on account of the fact that the Buddha talked of *Duḥkha* and the consideration of this at their hands might have led them to believe that Buddha's teaching is pessimistic. The other reason for taking *Śūnyatā* as emptiness is that '*Śūnyatā*' is understood in its bluntant literal sense giving rise to corresponding ontological import. This further helped the scholars to advance a view that the world is devoid of objects according to *Mādhyamikas*. Both these reasons, however, on deeper scrutiny turn out to be unsound. For, *Śūnyatā* as emptiness is not at all intended by the Buddha. But, as will be apparent from the sequel, it is also not understood by Nāgārjnna in this way. It is interesting, however, to note that the trend of understanding *Śūnyatā* literally is not an exclusively post Nāgārjuna intellectual trait. It is perfectly legitimate to hold that there might have been some of the predecessors as well as contemporaries of Nāgārjuna who might have also given this kind of interpretation to *Śūnyatā*. Otherwise it is very hard to understand the import of the summary of the argument of his *Pūrvapakṣin/s* that Nagarjuna outlines in the first half of the 24th chapter of the *Madhyamakaśāstra*. *Pūrvapaksin* of Nāgārjuna contends that if according to Nāgārjuna *Śūnyatā* is a tenable thesis then understanding *Śūnyatā* literally as Nāgārjuna appears to be prone to understand, not only four noble truths preached by the Buddha would make nonsense[10] but also that the entire world, no matter whether internal or external, would also be non-existent.[11] In the same vain all modes of ordinary actions, too, will meet the same fate.[12] In other words, understanding *Śūnyatā* literally there can be nothing worth the name that can legitimately be said to belong to the world.

In face of such an objection from *Pūrvapakṣin* Nāgārjuna considers it to be his first and foremost intellectual duty to tell in which sense *Śūnyatā* is not at all intended to be understood. He argues : one who understands *Śūnyatā* literally in this way not only does not understand the proper import of it but also fails to comprehend the very purpose for which it has been brought in vogue.[13] Elaborating the contention of Nāgārjuna, Candrakīrti tells us that such an interpretation of *Śūnyatā* originates out of imagination of *Pūrvapakṣin* who distorts and misapprehends its import.[14] He also tells us, quoting very approvingly *Madhyamakaśāstra* 24.18, that the expression *Śūnyatā* means exactly the same as the expression *Pratītya Samutpāda* means and not what the expression *abhāva* means.

Understanding the import of *Śūnyatā* in the latter sense amounts to distorting its import and consequently destroys the very purpose for which it has been invoked.[15] In an alike vein he argues that we do not at all wish to understand *Śūnyatā* in the sense of utter non-existence or void but rather in the sense of *Pratītya Samutpāda* and hence it is unjustifiable to bring those sorts of objections against our view, which would be proper had we understood *Śūnyatā* as we have been accused.[16]

Many more illustrations could be added to make out that Nāgārjuna does not intend to understand *Śūnyatā* literally. Nor does he wish to uphold the view that Buddha's philosophy is pessimistic. But it is the former issue that is our present concern. Understanding, then, *Śūnyatā* in the sense of *Pratītyasamutpāda* as Nāgārjuna understands it makes a world of difference to the import of the former. For, as pointed out in the former chapter, *Pratītya Samutpāda* rightly understood does not repudiate reality of everything; it rather upholds the reality of those and only those things which being genuinely ontological have rightful claim to inhabit the world. We also pointed out there that such things are discrete, mutually independent rather than interdependent and in so far as they do not have anything in common are isolated from each other, although in their being presented in succession or simultaneously they are related or connected with one another, though not for their existence or origination. Thus, understood *Śūnyatā* does not mean utter non-existence. It rather means taking those things alone to be real that are ontological in the strict and legitimate sense of the term. This is how *Śūnyatā* in its ontological aspect is said to converge upon *Pratītya Samutpāda* as a world-view and a theory of the world and things belonging to it. Candrakīrti tells us that such kind of things could be said to be *svalakṣaṇa* as we pointed out in the previous chapter. Understanding them to be so, they are discrete but not causally connected, changeable but not necessarily momentary, originating but not created by any agency like God. This meaning of *Śūnyatā* does not make Nāgārjuna's philosophy nihilistic; nor does it make Buddha's teaching pessimistic. It rather makes much better reading of the entire theory of *Pratītya Samutpāda* as will be apparent after we have accounted for other facets of *Śūnyatā*. It is not, thus, understanding *Śūnyatā* in the sense of negation that ontologicality of everything that is sought to be repudiated but rather that sort of relationship between it and *Pratītya Samutpāda* is intended to be brought out through which a proper philosophical position may come to be developed. As a matter of fact, it is interesting to observe, there are number of passages which show that about the reality of some objects Nāgārjuna as well as Candrakīrti were convinced and did not wish to founder their ontological status. It clearly shows that the view of scholars, that by *Śūnyatā* Nāgārjuna wanted to convey utter emptiness of the world, goes contrary to what Nāgārjuna has said about it and hence is totally untenable.

It may, however, be contended that *Śūnyatā* as Nāgārjuna intends to understand it need not necessarily be construed as non-existence of things themselves directly. But, nonetheless, the same conclusion could be said to be acceptable to him in another sense. As non-existence of things and emptiness of the world might turn out to be the features of his philosophy and to the extent to which this is possible, his philosophy cannot be totally said to be free from the charge of nihilism. Hence, without surrendering the characterization of Nāgārjuna's philosophy as nihilism, a strong supporter of nihilism may argue that though it 'could be granted that the world according to Nāgārjuna is structured by genuinely particular thing, yet a question remains : What do these things consist of? They have properties. This need not be understood as there are things and that they have properties. Instead, things that are said to be real could be taken to be composed of properties and nothing else. It means that everything is just a bundle of properties. There is nothing over and above these properties that can be said to be the case of a thing. So, if we analyse things into their properties ultimately there will not remain anything that can be said to be a thing. Further, each one of such ʃproperties is liable to vanish some time or the other as none of them is eternal and although all the properties of a thing may not cease to exist at a time but only some of them and in so far as such a spiral continuity of properties obtains, though none of the properties could be said to be a thing such a spiral convergence comes to be taken as a thing. But since there is nothing like a thing over and above totality of properties at any given time and since each one of such properties is likely to disappear non-existence of things and consequent emptiness of the world continues to be an official position of Nāgārjuna. Thus, Nāgārjuna's protest against total non-existence of things is weak and misleading and Candra-kīrti's heroic defence of it is untenable at heart. Therefore, although on the level of things one does not get emptiness, at least on the level of properties can we not rightly dispense with them and thereby say good-bye to things? Furthermore, since according to Nāgārjuna all *Dharmas* (properties) are *Śūnya*, it is no wonder, the charge continues, that according to him the world is empty and what he upholds in nihilism. Prima facie the argument seems to be appealing, but in a deeper analysis, it is full of difficulties : For, in order to hold this view one will have to show that everything according to Nāgārjuna is a bundle of properities and that there is nothing like a thing over and above such a bandle of properties. Now, as the matter stands we must very carefully note the following points : (a) Nāgārjuna does not repudiate everything and does not accept the world to be empty as argued above. (b) He does not understand a thing as a bundle of properties. He does not take partial or spiral convergence of properties to be a thing either. Understanding real to be that which cannot be otherwise than what it is, he does repudiate ontological status of many items which are said to enjoy such a status, as we shall see   But this, he does not do on the ground either that a thing under consideration is a bundle of properties or on the ground that each of the properties it has, is bound to cease to be, sometime or the other. As will be argued later, this he does on the ground that many of those things which are said to be ontologically real are not so because they do not enjoy the status they are said to enjoy. To say this is one thing and to say that this amounts to accepting bundle theory of a thing is quite another. The objection under consi-deration and defence of the characterization of Nāgārjuna's position as nihilism or emptiness is based on this presupposition which is questionable. Moreover, the danger in this explanation is that one gives primary occurrences to properties and secon-dary occurrences to things. Cognitively this may be so, in so far as we cognize properties first and things of which they are properties later. But what is cognitively prior need not neces-sarily so ontologically as well. Again, properties are always **properties of something and cannot be given an independent** status to them. One may fu ther come to put forth such a view out of the confusion between properties of possession and properties of attribution. Properties of attribution are always contingent. But properties of possession—which are invariably inseparable from the things and which are structurally related with them—cannot be said to be so contingent. That is, those properties in the absence of which the thing does not remain that thing, alone are real properties. Rest of the properties are contingent, or at least do not determine the nature and structure of a thing It is such properties which Nāgārjuna calls *niḥsvābhāvika*.[17] Such properties are *Śūnya*; not all properties. Therefore, the contention that, since according to Nāgārjuna there are only properties and no things, his view is nihilistic is neither justifiable nor warrantable.

We argued earlier that *Śūnyatā* at the hands of Nāgā juna needs to be understood both positively and negatively. Positively understood, in its ontological aspect, we argued, converges upon the world and world-view that surfaces provided we understand *Pratītyasamutpāda* the way it needs to be understood according to Nāgārjuna. But, as pointed out in the previous chapter, *Pratītya Samutpāda* can be understood commonsensically, where everything is said to be causally related with something or the other and all the things that are said to belong to the world are taken to enjoy an equal ontological status. Now, in so far as *Śūnyatā* is said to be related with *Pratītya Samutpāda*, it could be said to be so related no matter which version of *Pratītya Samutpāda* we accept. Thus understood, *Śūnyatā* could be taken to be a tool on the basis of which any version of *Pratītya Samutpāda* would be defensible. Such a position is obviously not acceptable to Nāgārjuna. He rather understands the problem differently. According to him of the two aspects of *Śūnyatā* ontologically understood—viz. positive and negative—the former is connected with the rightly understood *Pratītya Samutpāda* while the latter is connected with the commonsensical understanding of *Pratītya Samutpāda*. In its former aspect those and only those features of the world that genuinely belong to it are sought to be justified, inclusive of the world that is genuinely ontological and those things belonging to it which enjoy such a status. In the latter aspect all those features of the world, that sort of world and those sort of things are sought to be repudiated and our world-view cleansed of the rubbish which cannot genuinely be said to be real. It is the reality of only such items that is sought to be questioned. But it is precisely this aspect of *Śūnyatā* at the hands of the Buddha and Nāgārjuna that comes to be misunderstood and misinterpreted. Now, it comes to be held that since the reality of some items is sought to be questioned and since they are sought to be repudiated, reality of every possible item must be sought to be questioned and hence the only view that is intended to be upheld is that of Nihilism—directly or indirectly. In its former version no items would be admitted to be real, while on the latter version reality of items said to be real will be shown to be derivative and hence questionable. In any case, therefore, Nāgārjuna's intention must be to advance nihilism in whichever form it could be respectable.

It is this which Nāgārjuna is disputing, saying that it is not his intention to repudiate anything and everything. He neither wants to say that nothing is real nor does he wish to hold that no feature is a structural and constitutive feature of the world or of things belonging to it. He however, does mean to hold that everything that is held to be real cannot be so held and every feature that we believe to be belonging to the world is not a structural feature of it. To say this, does not amount to upholding nihilism as a philosophical position. Thus, by the employment of the notion of *Śūnyatā*, Nāgārjuna never meant that there are no things as well as properties, which not being independent are contingent and derivative. He employs *Śūnyatā* positively to convey that there are particular things in the world. None of them are eternal. All arise sometime, continue to be for sometime and perish away eventually in the course of time. Such particular things are given simultaneously or in succession. In the latter case, we experience the phenomena of flow. Such a flow indeed has many things belonging to it and they also could be said to be connected, though not necessarily causally. The flow or *Santān* implies that there are things and they are given in succession. But it neither establishes that the preceeding thing is a cause of subsequent thing, nor the subsequent thing is the effect of its antecedent. Thus, an employment of *Śūnyatā* on ontological level serves two purposes : i) It acknowledges that there are particular things in the world and ii) It seeks to do away with the otherwise proliferative growth of real objects alongwith their properties which are taken to be there but do not legitimately enjoy the status of being real.

It seems to us that there is another equally prominent reason behind the advocacy of *Śūnyatā* on ontological level before *Mādhymikas* in general and Nāgārjuna in particular. It is to repudiate the existence of 'self' which is the principal shaft around which many of those ontological and epistemological issues, taken normally to be philosophically interesting, revolve. Such issues are taken to be genuine because reality of self is taken to be unquestionable on commonsensical understanding. The general outline of the argument, on commonsensical under-standing, in defence of the existence of self, is this : i) 'there is a self ontically existing', for there is *saṁsāra*. Further, there is *duḥkha* and unless the self and activities undertaken by self are accepted, we cannot make a philosophically satisfactory sense of *saṁsāra* as well as *duḥkha*. This is especially the case because in the absence of self many of our experiences cannot be made sense of. Nor could many of our commonsensical modes of action and feeling be given the kind of legitimacy that they deserve. ii) Secondly, in common parlance, we talk about actions, doer of actions, fruit of actions, enjoyer or sufferer of fruit of actions etc. We take all these to be real. But they are all superstrata. Now, if they are real then there is no reason to hold why that which underlies them should not be taken to be real Such a substratum is self. Thus, our states, feelings, experiences, cognitions, conations, commonsensical expressions and the entire conceptual framework that it brings forward is presumed to be real and to be able to give legitimacy to all of them, it is held that there must be an entity called self without which our actions, emotions, feelings, cognitions etc. cannot be made sense of. Accordingly, anything and everything that is taken to be designation of a commonsensically significant expre-ssion is taken to be real and hence belonging to the world as a legitimate component of its furniture.

Such a view brings forth two crucial difficulties; one, it presupposes a certain kind of relationship between language and world, and we shall have an occasion to probe into it at a later stage of our argument in this chapter. Two, it also presupposes a certain relationship between human experience and the world and the things as they are given to us. It further presupposes a certain priority relationship such that whatever we experience is uniquely determined by the corresponding kind of thing that is real. For, unless such a thing is real, it would make no sense to say that it determines our experience of it. This being the case, our experiences have to be taken to be an important clue to our discovery of those things which are real. Both these assumptions Nāgārjuna questions, quite rightly. For the present we shall concentrate on the latter assumption. The fundamental objection that Nāgārjuna raises against the view under consideration is :   What are we going to make the basis of our philosophical investigations and scrutiny? On what basis are we hoping to certify our philosophically significant views? Everything that we are prone to take to be real, on whatever commonsensical consideration, may not be so as a matter of fact. Likewise, if experience is taken to be the basis of something to be taken to be real, then in our quest of real items that belong to the world we may come to include not only those which legitimately belong to it but may more as well. But if all those items are admitted as not only real but also as genuinely real things then it will create an ontological slum resulting into a disastrous consequence of over-populated world and such a world can hardly be said to be philosophically interesting. Such a world has to be the one that fulfils a philosophically interesting criterion and that such a world is philosophically interesting simply because it is most close to commonsically accepted world cannot be such a criterion. Nāgā juna and Chandrakīrti, therefore, scrutinize the commonsensical pattern of world alongwith its so-called real items with the help of the powerful methodological tool—*Śūnyatā* and point out their non-obtainability so far their reality in the strict sense of the term is concerned Candrakīrti on these issues argues that granting that there is *saṁsāra* gives rise to further difficulties. For, since *saṁsāra* is not something that is real, because it is non-independent and derivative, presupposing it to be real we are also forced to accept reality of that which ir posterior to *saṁsāra*,[18] as also of that of which it is a consequent. But on what grounds do we take that which is prior to *saṁsāra* to be real? Thus, reality of *saṁsāra* itself is questionable and hence on its basis reality of self cannot be said to be defensible[19], If it is said that there is self because there are experiences of pleasure and pain, then, too, the argument remains philosophically uninteresting. For, in that case, we do not grant independent existence to self and call it real, but rather on the ground that it is pre-supposed by our experience of pain. We can hope to justify reality of self in this way provided our experience of pain at least were taken to be real because it is independent. But its reality itself being questionable, the very argument that there is self because there is pain does not remain tenable.[20]   The number of ways in which reality of self is sought to be justified turn out to be such that each one of them, on closer scrutiny, turns out to be untenable for the very simple reason that in each one of those ways we come to base reality of self upon the reality of something which itself is questionable. Therefore, though in common parlance, we talk about *samsāra*, *duḥkha* or *self* yet none of them could be taken as genuinely real things.[21]   Reality of self cannot be said to be justifiable on the basis of the reality of action of whatever kind either. For, if reality of self is sought to be justified on the ground that it is the doer of action then, too, there is a trouble. This merely amounts to shifting burden of the justification of reality of self one step backward. But what about the ontological status of actions themselves? Are they independent and hence real? This cannot be and whatever explanation of the reality of action we advance remains frought with difficulties.[22]   Thus, reality of self even on this count, too, remains questionable.

As reality of self remains questionable so too reality of states of things remains questionable. On what ground do we say states of things to be real? Is it because they are independent? Or rather is it because our impressions of them are taken to be real? But what about the reality of impressions itself? Can we say that impressions are real because they are independent? Not at all.[23] Nor can we say that states are real since they are caused by contacts between our senses and states. For, there is no way to hold reality of such contacts on the ground of their independent existence.[24] Nothing could likewise be taken to be genuinely given to us unless it can be shown to be of such kind that it cannot be otherwise i.e. unless it can be shown to be non-derivative.[25] Any feature that is derivative cannot be said to be native, structural and constitutive.[26] Thus, nativity of a feature would indicate incapability of its being severed from that of which it is a feature, it being ungenerated out of or because of something.[27] Thus understood, many of the states and the features of things as also things that are taken to be real, cannot, on philosophically justifiable basis, be taken to be real, although commonsensically they are taken to be so. They are not sought to be denied or their reality is not sought to be questioned arbitrarily, but because they do not fulfil the criterion of anything being taken to be genuinely real.

Lastly, let us take into account Nāgārjuna's views on time. He inquires into reality of time not independently of any context. It is often held that various states of things that we experience are real because their reality is derivative from that we time, especially because such states of things as are taken to be real come to be given to us in terms of temporal priority and postiriority. Such would have been the case provided time were real in the genuine sense of the term. That is, if independence, underivativeness, unrelatively, unchangeability etc. were structural features of it.[28] But since this itself is questionable, it can also not be said that those states and features of things which are temporally given to us are real. There he argues that though we talk about time in everyday transactions, yet time is a mere notion coined for the purpose of explanation of things. So it has only explanatory status. The division of time in past, present and future, again, is anthropocentric, which is brought into practice for our own convenience. Further, we say that a particular state of a thing we come to know, say, at time T_1 or T_2; but it is a matter of sheer coincidence and there is no necessity involved in it i.e. things can be said to be real though they are not presented in terms of temporal priority or posteriority. Moreover, reality of time is also questionable on above-mentioned counts. Therefore, philosophically considered, time or division of time cannot be regarded to have ontological status,[29] and can be easily dispensed with. On the same line Candrakīrti repudiates ontological status of contact (*saṁsarga*),[30] coming and going of things (*sambhavavibhava*)[31], co-operative conditions (*sahakāri kārana*),[32] *Tathāgata*[33] *bhāvasantati*[34] etc. on the ground that none of them is genuinely ontologically real. This is not to deny their role and importance in commonsensical world-view,

Nor does it amount to question their role as categories used for the purpose of explanation. It also does not amount to saying that each of them is a bundle of Nonsense.

In this entire investigation into the ontological status of many of the items regarded to be antological on the basis of commonsensical consideration about them, there are certain points of very crucial significance involved, overlooking which appears to have led many a scholars to advance such views about Nāgārjuna's philosophy that are at variance from the central tenet of it. First, as we pointed out earlier, *Śūnyatā* as a methodological tool that Nāgārjuna employs is essentially a janus-faced one in the sense that it has positive and negative aspects of it and that it is not intended to be wielded in the same way with regard to both the aspects of it. This is so in each one of the three principal domains in which Nāgārjuna wields and exploits it—ontology, epistemology and language. Limitting for the present to its exploitation in the domain of ontology, it is again important to remember that *Pratītya Samutpāda*, too, in turn could be understood in two principal ways—as Nāgārjuna intends to understand and as it is commonsensically understood. The positive aspect of *Śūnyatā* is sought to be correlated with the former; while the negative aspect with the latter—the former correlation is for the defence while latter for repudiation. This is often not understood clearly. Secondly, those items whose reality is repudiated are not dismissed arbitrarily. A criterion of anything that is real in the genuine sense of the term is formulated—both with regard to thing and its feature. Anything that fails to fulfil that criterion alone is sought to be questioned. The wielding of *Śūnyatā* as a methodological tool in the ontological domain of inquiry and elsewhere, as we shall see, is backed by conceptual consistency and Nāgārjuna is prepared to go alongwith it wherever and as far as it leads. But the world-view he wants to put forth is not sought to be defended on the ground of consistency alone, and thus there is no circularity in the endeavour undertaken by him. That no the criterion of reality that is accepted, being too stringent, many of those items that are normally considered to be real lose their claim to reality is a consequence which we are not accustomed to go along. But Nāgārjuna has not signed a contract with us that he will accept only such a criterion of reality according to which everything we take to be real shall remain so. In other words, Nāgārjuna cannot be forced to accept a weaker criterion of reality unless it can be shown that the one he accepts leads to the kind of inconsistency which any respectable philosophical position must avoid at any cost, if it is to be respectable. Philosophical scrutiny is not always bound to necessarily go along what is commonsensically considered to be interesting and tenable. This is again quite often forgotten. Thirdly, the reality of those things and states or features of them that is sought to be disputed is not sought to be disputed solely on the ground that none of them is genuinely real because none of them fulfils the criterion of genuine reality. Nonetheless, accepting derivative and hence non-genuine reality of something or the other, in the face of Nāgārjuna's formidable argument against it, it is sought to be argued that their reality need not be repudiated, as Nāgārjuna attempts to do. For, each one of them is said to be an outcome of something else that is a necessary condition of the outcome or emergence of the former kind of thing. For instance, *samsāra*, *duḥkha*, experiences etc. are said to be such necessary conditions of the emergence of self, and it is this kind of relation between them that is said to confer reality on the items that is held to be emerging in this way. It is this kind of argument that Nāgārjuna questions tenability of and that too on two principal grounds : (a) one, under such circumstances it is the intellectual responsibility of the person who puts forth such an argument to establish that an item, which is considered to be a necessary condition of the emergence of an item whose reality is derivative; is such a necessary condition not because it is conventional to take it that way, or because it is presumed, but rather because it fulfils the criterion of a necessary condition, viz. when it is present, effect arises, and when it is absent, effect simply does not arise. In so far as this is not done the claim that some item is a necessary condition for the emergence of some other item is questionable and unreliable. For instance, if time is said to be necessary condition of constitutive and structural features of a thing, then it will have to be shown that without time such features of a thing just cannot be. Since such an exercise is not undertaken claims of this kind that are advanced do not remain philosophically respectable. (b) Two, granted that reality of A is derivative, and hence it is said to emerge from B. Or A is said to be real on account of B as a necessary condition of it. Nonetheless, the problem of reality of B does continue to chase us. On what ground are we going to say that B is real? Is it, again, saying that B is real because it emerges from C as its necessary condition? If so, B is not accepted to be real because it fulfils the criterion of being real but on some other ground and that itself is a matter of dispute between Nāgārjuna and his *Pūrvapakṣin.* Moreover, what about the fact that such a line of justifying reality of something will lead to an infinite regress? Instead of this will it not be proper to formulate a criterion or criteria of something being real and by applying it to take those and only those items to be real which fulfils the conditions laid down by the criterion so formulated? It is this that Nāgārjuna is insisting upon. But it is precisely this that his *Pūrvapakṣin* fails to comply with. Under such circumstances he follows the course of misunderstand and distorting what Nāgārjuna wants to uphold and defend. This kind of unfair means naturally comes to be opposed by Nāgārjuna and his commentator Candrakīrti and quite rightly. Very often, at the hands of scholars, this is, again, lost sight of and as a result they appear to give such interpretation to his philosophy which are at variance from the principal tenets of it.

This is how Nāgārjuna and Candrakirti repudiate the realistic approach of commonsensical understanding as it is detrimental to tenable philosophic deliberations. Nāgārjuna's criticism of realistic approach is not carried out for the sake of criticism. Rather, he carries out such an unavoidable job as the commonsensical approach not only gives rise to proliferative ontology but it is also far away from the teaching of the Buddha as it distorts the real picture of the world rather than reveals it.

Thus on taking the world to be full of genuinely real and the so-called real things commonsensical view of *Pratītya Samutpāda* gives us such a nature and structure of the world that is beset with many philosophical shortcomings. When *Śūnyatā* is wielded as a methodological tool, to do away with the artificial growth of such a world and when the so-called real entities are substracted from the totality of the world, the remnant world and the world given through *Pratītyasamutpāda* properly understood converge upon each other. It is in this sense that

Pratītyasamntpāda and *Śūnyatā* are equated many times.[35]   This
is how Nāgārjuna points out non-obtainability of those things
which are not genuinely real with the help of *Śūnyatā* as a
methodological tool employed in ontological domain of inquiry.
But in so far as the items that are genuinely real are particular
and discrete Nāgārjuna's coming to wield *Śūnyatā* as a methodological tool in ontology could also be said to be leading to yet
another consequence-viz., formulation and defence of a nominalistic ontology. This, too, very often does not appear to have
been understood. With this we proceed to consider the way
Śūnyatā, as a methodological tool, comes to be exploited by
Nāgārjuna with regard to questions concerning human knowledge.

Śūnyatā : *Epistemological Aspect*

We saw that in considering utilization and exploitation
of *Śūnyatā* in ontological domain of inquiry Nāgārjuna's understanding of it comes to be opposed on the basis of two positions.
On the one hand, nihilism which is correlative with literal interpretation of *Śūnyatā* and, on the other, an attempt to confer
ontological status on every item that commonsensically comes to
be regarded as real and which is correlative with commonsensical
interpretation of *Pratītyasamutpāda*. Analogously, with regard
to exploitation of *Śūnyatā* as a methodological tool in epistemological domain of inquiry Nāgārjuna's view about human knowledge is attempted to be opposed in two principal ways : (a) one,
on the basis of overwhelming scepticism - both facts and warrant
challenging-according to which nothing is knowable and even if
something is taken to be knowable, our knowledge of it just
cannot be certain, and (b) two, in so far as ordinarily we do not
dispute our knowledge claims, all those knowledge-claims which
are ordinarily taken to be respectable must also remain so in a
philosophical scrutiny about them and any philosophical inquiry
that deviates from ordinarily uncontested knowledge-claims is
epistemologically sinful and therefore does not deserve that
respect which it demands. On this view every knowledge claim
that is ordinarily taken to be respectable must continue to be
taken so and accordingly even a moderate scepticism about such
claims is not respectable. We have to see how Nāgārjuna's
exploitation of *Śūnyatā* in epistemological inquiry stands in face

of these two kinds of oppsitions to it, without succumbing to either of them. It is to this consideration that we now turn.

Coming first to the second way. According to it every bit of information that is commonsensically considered to be respectable must remain so in a philosophical scrutiny, perhaps because a philosophical investigation worth the name cannot afford to deviate from commonsense. Against this view Nāgārjuna argues that neither the Buddha nor he himself wish to defend and warrant what is commonsensically taken to be certifiable piece of information. For, doubts and misconceptions generated but it need to be examined and how much of it and to what extent is tenable needs to be investigated.[36] Moreover, it is not a pledge of the Buddha or of Nāgārjuna that they would put forth their view on the basis of what is ¦ commonsensically accepted.[37] Rather, they wished to bring to our notice how much of what is so accepted is untenable and on what grounds. Thus, they did not wish to argue that everything that is commonsensically accepted must be tenable; rather their aim was to systematize that commonsensically accepted information which is tenable in the light of a philosophical theory.[38] This being the case, no information, according to Nāgārjuna, would be reliable just because it is taken to be uncontested commonsensically and hence tenable. Such an information needs to be investigated and on the basis of such an inquiry it is not unlikely that in some cases the facts themselves, taken to be trustworthy, may turn out to be different from what they are taken to be, while in some cases information certifying ground itself may be unreliable. Philosophically interesting inquiry in human knowledge cannot hope to proceed with a pledge that it shall not deviate from commonsense, come what may. If it proceeds this way then many of philosophical views would turn out to be of questionble reliability. Hence, such an inquiry can at the most begin from investigation into commonsensically accepted knowledge with a view to find out whether and to what extent it could be said to be reliable. This is precisely what the Buddha and Nāgārjuna intend to undertake. We may not dispute our knowledge claims because they are dear to us and since they are advanced by us. But this in itself cannot be taken to be a philosophically interesting basis of not contesting them. Such an investigation must proceed impartially. In the absence of this we are more likely to end up with subjective opinions which by no means could be substituted for knowledge.

Turning to the first way. Here Nāgārjuna appears to argue that if the kind of scepticism-fact or warrant-challenging-that is sought to be advanced were based on respectable basis matter would have been different. Unfortunately it is advanced on the basis of distortion and misinterpretation of what the Buddha laboured to put forth or what Nāgārjuna wished to upheld. *Mādhyamikas* in general and Nāgārjuna in particular do not intend to deny every item, rather they wish to deny those and only those items which cannot be taken to be things in so far as they cannot be said to be satisfying criterion of being a genuinely real thing,[39] Moreover, in so far as *Mādhyamikas* are interested in knowing the nature of things as they are structured and constituted, rather than as we experience them, it cannot be said that they wish to repudiate any and every short of fact.[40] This being the case, a whole-scale charge, Nāgārjuna argues, on us that we wish to adhere to facts or worrant challenging scepticism or that we intend to repudiate and contest every commonsensically accepted knowledge claim is injustifiable.[41] We are certainly interested, he continues, in certification issue of human knowledge. But there we do not wish to go about arbitrarily. Our attempt will all along be to accept those knowledge-claims that are acceptable and reject those that are not so.[42] The two epistemological positions - viz., nothing whatever is knowable and no knowledge-claim is certifiable and each of our knowlege claim is reliable-are to be judiciously avoided as two untehable extremes.

If the certifiability of knowledge-claims about things is necessarily connected with the obtainability of things about which the knowledge claims are certifiable as well as warrantable which are made about genuinely real things, since genuinely real things alone are obtainable. It seems to us that critics of Nāgārjuna appear to have considerably confused between 'knowing' and 'communicating'. According to *Mādhyamikas* there may be no difficulty in 'knowing' or 'cognizing' ; it may perhaps arise in connection with 'communicating'. But this latter kind of difficulty arises because of defectiveness of language and such a kind of defectiveness of language or complaints about it cannot be made basis of saying that Nāgārjuna is out to repudiate any knowledge claim whatever and hence that he is a sceptic.

On epistemological level, thus, *Śūnyatā* does not mean an emptiness of human knowledge. Rather, it empties misplead claims of scepticism. *Śūnyatā*, therefore, on epistemological count neither means an impossibility of knowledge nor does it mean absolute unwarrantability as well as unjustifiability of knowledge claims. Nor even does it embrace realistic approach that every knowledge claim is warrantable. It, rather, emphasises that certain knowledge claims are warrantable, while certain others are not. Just as Nāgārjuna admits that there are particular things on ontological level, so too, according to him there is knowledge of those particular things on epistemological level. Thus, an employment of *Śūnyatā* on epistemological level as a methodological tool, washes away both the claims that "there is no knowledge at all" and "everything is knowable" advanced by a overwhelming sceptic and a realist respectively, and upholds a position between the two that certain knowledge claims are in principle and fact warrantable.

In epistemology, if that kind of knowledge is called knowledge which is certifiable then it must be knowledge of those items which truly belong to the world. Rest items of so-called knowledge turn out to be 'opinions' (*dṛṣṭis*) and need to be given up. Nāgārjuna by employing *Śūnyatā* on this level wants to nullify all such items of knowledge which are of the nature of opinions.[43] Thus, just as in the domain of ontology Nāgārjuna avoids the two extremes of utter nihilism and naive realism through the employment of methodological weapon of *Śūnyatā*, so too, in epistemological inquiry using the same weapon, he judiciously avoids the two extremes of utter scepticism and commonsensical realism. Again, just as in the former case he makes *Śūnyatā* to converge on legitimately understood *Pratītya Samutpāda*, so too, in the latter case he brings out relation between those things which genuinely are there and our knowledge of them. In other words, knowledge of those and only those things is taken to be reliable which as a matter of fact are there and it goes without saying that such things are given to us by rightly understood *Pratītya Samutpāda*. In this way, even through the gateway of epistemological inquiry we return to the same principal issue of the intimate relationship between *Pratītya Samutpāda* and *Śūnyatā*. It is an ingenuity of Nāgārjuna that he is able to impress upon us the same crucially important point in different alternative ways and through undertaking a philosophically interesting inquiry in more than one domains of investigations. Now, it remains to be seen how Nāgārjuna employs the notion of *Śūnyatā* on the logico-linguistic plane. It is to this consideration that we now turn.

Śūnyatā : *Logico Linguistic Aspect*

a) *Sarvadharmaśūnyatā* :

It is not a confidential matter that we use language for communication Resorting to such a kind of language we either say that a particular thing has or does not have a particular characteristic or *dharma* or a quality. The kind of language which we employ for the description of the things is such that it itself possesses subject-predicate model.[44] Without referring to the nature of predicates it will be noticed that Nāgārjuna points out that not only predicate creates problems for us but the very mould of predicative language is prone to engender certain problems for us.[45] For instance, subject-predicate form of the language employs certain predicates. They are believed to be predicates of things. But by the very nature of the case, each predicate that we employ is a predicate of a class of a thing, i.e. in order to stand as a predicate it must be applicable to more than one thing of that kind at a time. Through and on account of such a state of affair we come to hold that the things under consideration have some properties that are shareable and common and in so far as they possess such properties they resemble each other and yet differ from one another. But since, according to Nāgārjuna, as we pointed out, earlier, the things in the world are uniquely particular such that no two of them are similar or identical one cannot hope to ascribe any predicate or *dharma* to bring out the feature of that kind of thing. For, *dharma* signifies only a shareable and not a unique feature of a thing. Thus, our attempt of describing a particular thing with the help of predicates, characteristics as *dharmas* fails to describe

the thing under consideration; rather, it distorts the nature of it.
Thus, we are unable to make use of predicative language discrip-
tively not because things do not possess qualities but simply
because any predicate qua predicate, is intended to bring out
common, shareable or similar characteristics of things and since
no two things have anything in common and since they are not
similar, not to say identical, we fail to obtain such things to
whom we can successfully ascribe predicates and thereby describe them predicatively. This being the case the entire range
of predicative language is utterly unsuitable to bring out the
nature of genuinely real unique things.[46]

One may perhaps rule out the predicative language altogether by saying that it is incompetent to bring out the peculiarity
and particularity of each one of the bare particular thing. For,
if all the expressions in our language are suitable to bring out
shareable and common feature or property and if no expression
can be used to describe uniquely particular thing then we shall
have no other alternative linguistic machinery with which we
shall be in a position to bring out nature of such particular
objects descriptively. Instead, in order not to turn so radical
in our consideration can we not say that predicative language
is unsuited to bring out the functional features of things but not
so much the structural feature of them, That is, instead of
summarily dismissing descriptive language as thoroughly impo-
tent to describe the nature of uniquely particular objects does
this kind of via-media not seen to be worth considering?

Nāgārjuna, here too, dismisses the proposed via-media by
saying that no matter whether we are talking of structural or
functional features of things predicatively intended to be brought
out, in so far it is a predicate and since any predicate, which
we employ, brings out either similar or common character of
things and since no two genuinely real things have any common
or similar property or *dharma*, there is no propriety in saying
that such a predicative language can at least bring out structural
feature of a thing though not functional one. But if they were
to be structurally similar no one would have said that they are
uniquely particular. That they are uniquely particular itself is
sufficient to hold that they are not structurally similar. Since
everything that genuinely is, is of the nature of *svalakṣaṇa* and

since no *svalakṣaṇa* can be thought of as having characteristics or *dharmas* similar to or in common with other *svalakṣaṇa* things, all predicates indicative of commonality are inapplicable to genuinely particular things, given either simultaneously or in succession. Such unique things could not have arisen from a stuff that commonly infiltrates each one of them either. Besides, how do we know that a particular *dharma* which we ascribe to a particular thing is a *dharma* of that thing alone? That is, unless there is a certainty that a given thing alone has the given *dharma* our describing a particular thing with that particular *dharma* cannot be methodologically as well as logically justifiable.[47] Similarly, there is no hard and fast rule which would justify our ascribing any *dharma* to any particular thing, and not any other. Therefore, it follows that any *dharma* which is descriptively used is necessiated either by our expectations or by our explanation, but in none of the case they are necessary to understand the nature of the genuinely particular thing presented to us. Thus, *Śūnyatā* one phase of its use on logico-linguistic level amounts to accepting total incompetence of predicative language, where every predicate signifies a common property, descriptively used to bring out the nature of a uniquely partcular thing.[48]

Coming to the analysis of the nature of predicates or *dharmas*, can we say that there are predicates independently existing apart from the things? The word *dharma* is derived from the root 'dhṛ' which means to hold and then *dharma* is that which holds something.[49] But in that case *dharma* becomes logically prior to the thing of which it is a *dharma* and in this context it gets an independent status. But it cannot be acceptable. We never perceive thing and its *dharma* as separable entities. We never experience *Pṛthivi* and *Kāthiṇya* — its *dharma* separately but *Kāthiṇya* which is inseparable from *Pṛthivi* such that if it is removed from *Pṛthivi*, there does not remain anything like *Pṛthivi*. So, what is given to us is always a particular state of a thing including inseparable *dharma* and not an independent *dharma*. Therefore, one of the purposes behind the employment of *Śūnyatā*, Nāgārjuna contends, is to point out *niḥsvabhāvyatā* of *dharmas*.[50] Hence every *dharma* which we ascribe to things on commonsensical understanding is *Pratītyasamutpanna*; every *pratītyasamutpanna* thing lacks *svabhāva*; whatever lacks *svabhāva* is *niḥsvabhāva* and whatever is *niḥsvabhāva* is *Śūnya*. Therefore all *dharmas* are *Śūnya* [51]

From this analysis of predicates, with the help of methodological tool—*Śūnyatā*, one may be tempted to argue that the picture of predicatively descriptive language, as Nāgārjuna puts it before us, leads us to draw the conclusion that even though there are genuinely real things the knowledge of such particulars is not and cannot be imparted linguistically, and hence it is not communicable. But such a view cannot be tenable. For, Nāgārjuna never points out an incommunicability of our knowledge in any language whatever, rather he points out its incommunicability through the language we normally have due to its inherently defective nature. He says that in so far as the present linguistic pattern is concerned, it is more prone to generality or commonality rather than to particularity That is, it cannot express the peculiar nature of genuinely real things. Further, if it is expected that our linguistic tool be such that it should express the certified true knowledge then, our present language unfortunately lacks the necessary competence to carry out this job. This does not mean that thoughts are utterly incommunicable. To say that thoughts are utterly incommunicable is one thing and to say that our present language is unsuited for this purpose is quite another. It is the latter which the Buddhists like Nāgārjuna upheld. By that they do not at all intend to rule out the possibility of thought-communication.

b) *Sarvapadārthaśūnyatā*

As it is already pointed out, the aim behind the employment of *Śūnyatā* on logico-linguistic level is more powerful and is directed towards countering the criticism of Buddha's teaching within the framework of realism. As Nāgārjuna is critical about the notion of *dharma*, so too, he is critical about the status of concepts and categorical frames. Here he argues that as we take *dharmas* and characteristics to be real and independently existing so, too, we take concepts and categories and employ them as explanatory devices in our coming to know the peculiar and particular thing. But it does not in any way mean that a particular conceptual frame is fied down with particular thing. Nor is it the case that a particular thing dictates a particular categorical and/or conceptual frame, to be utilized for its description. Concepts and categories are methodological tools and are certainly important in so far as the employment of our present language for the description of such things is concerned. But one cannot, from this, maintain that they are so necessary, that they are part and parcel of the furniture of the world, that our not recognizing them to be so leads to rob the things of their ontological content. Given things as bare particulars and genuinely real as no *dharma* is helpful in bringing out the nature of particular things within the frame of language, so too, are not the conceptual and categorical frames. For, by their very nature, they can be utilized profitably with regard to things that have shareable features. Thus, Nāgārjuna and Candrakīrti attempt to put forward *sarvapadārtha śūnyatā* not only to denounce the ontological status of *Padārthas* but also to point out that they are equally unsuitable and unhelpful to bring out the nature of uniquely particular and genuinely real objects.[52]

Let us take a stock of Nāgārjuna's argument against *padārthas* to understand the principal point he is urging us to take into account. He is not saying, as may be thought, that in our commonsensical accounts of things, that we presume to be given, we do not utilize and exploit *Padārthas*. Nor does he hold that in such an account of things they do not serve even on explanatory purpose. His crucial contention is that, to begin with *Padārthas* are not ontological entities. Secondly, the concepts and categories we normally make use of are intimately tied with and remain inseparable from the kind of language we generally use for our everyday communication. In so far as we are nurtured and brought up in the atmosphere of such a language is itself no basis to say that no other language can be used for communicational purpose except the one we normally use, no matter whatever kind of world, as a matter of fact, is given to us. Thirdly, that the kind of concepts and categories we normally employ go well with the generally accepted version of *Pratītyasamutpāda* is in itself no ground to say that sort of understanding of *Pratītyasamutpāda* alone is philosophically interesting and reliable. Fourthly, our concepts and categories are very intimately connected with properties that are shareable and common. But if the things given to us are unique and they lack shareable structural features then such properties which bring out their shareable features would be unsuitable. Consequently, that sort of conceptual and categorical framework that is in accord with such properties and commonsensical understanding of Pratītyasamutpāda cannot be said to be suitable for our being able to communicate about those things—uniquely particular—that proper understanding of *Pratītya Samutpāda* makes available to us. It is on this background that the view of Nāgārjuna, that in so far as no *Padārtha* is naturally connected with kind of things that are given[53] it makes no sense to say that there are any *Padārthas*,[54] needs to be understood. He, on the same ground, does not accept the plea from his *Pūrvapakṣin* that the *Padārthas* may at least be conceded to have relative natural connection with the kind of things that are as a matter of fact given to us.[55] It is sufficient for the present purpose to consider *sarvapadārthaśūnyatā*. Let us now turn to the account of *Sarvabhāvaśūnyatā*.

c)   *Sarvabhāvaśūnyatā* :

There still remains one aspect of *Śūnyatā* to be considered and it is concerning Nāgārjuna's treatment of *Śūnyatā* of the states of things (*bhāvas*). Sometimes it is held that as Nāgārjuna advocates *Sarvadharmaśūnyatā* and *sarvapadārthaśūnyatā* by saying that all *dharmas* are *niḥsvābhāvika* or no conceptual and categorical model is *svābhāvika* to the uniquely particular things, similarly he must be upholding the view that all *bhāvas* (of things) are *niḥsvābhāvika*. To this Candrakīrti replies that we cannot hope to maintain such a view that all *bhāvas* are *niḥsvābhāvika*. He further says that we indeed talk about unreality of states of things but that does not mean that we intend to say that all *bhāvas* are *niḥsvābhāvika*. Whenever we put forth such a view, it means (1) those states of things which are derivative are *niḥsvābhāvika*, which are taken for granted as real on the basis of our illusory experience or expectations or dispositions etc. or those which are taken to be natural to things on the basis of our commonsensical understanding of *Paatītyasamutpāda*. For instance, our perceiving particular state of a thing in illusion or our perceiving a particular state of a woman in picture are bare *niḥsvābhāvika*[56] (2) When we advocate *niḥsvābhāvikatā* of states of things it means that states have no independent states apart from the things of which they are states i.e. genuine states are always inseparably and structurally connected with the things. So if anybody is to hold that states are independent of things then such states are unreal.

What is meant, then, by *naisvābhāvya* of *bhāvas* is not that any *bhāva* is *niḥsvabhāva* but rather that any *bhāva* that is *Pratītyasamu'panna* is *niḥsvabhāva*.[57] If, however, any *bhāva* is structural, non-artificial,[58] unrelative then alone can it be *svābhāvika* and can be rightly said to belong to unique particular things given to us by rightly understood *Pratītyasamutpāda*. In other words, what is intended to be said is that all states are not real[59] or that each and every state is not structural to a thing.[60] Thus, through employing *śūnyatā* on all those *bhāvas* which are taken to be real in accordance with commonsensical understanding of *Pratītya Samutpāda* we are expected to be brought back to the correlations between rightly understood *Pratītyasumutpāda* and *Śūnyatā* as a methodological tool to elaborate and defend it.

Thus, on the logico-linguistic plane *Śūnyatā* as a methodological tool is employed to show that given the kind of language we normally have along with its conceptual and categorial frame, has two featues : (i) that all expressions in it can be used to talk about more than one objects at a time and (ii) Such expressions and the concepts they signify cannot enable us to refer to or describe things truly ontological. They, rather are related to objects which are not genuinely ontological. The employment of such a language further presupposes, perhaps, that there is one—one correspondence between world and words and thus accepts a kind of name theory of meaning. This is how we come to be misled, Nāgārjuna tells us, by subject-predicate mould of language and we fail to make those distinctions which are not only methodologically important but also philosophically interesting.

Logically and methodologically, in this way, *Śūnyatā* is aimed at pointing out incapability of our normal predicates (*dharma*), predicative language, conceptual and categorial frames (*Padārtha*) and states and modalities (*bhāva*) to bring out the nature of uniquely particular things.[61] It is also intended to show that the linguistic tool that is at our disposal brings with it more problems than it solves. It is indeed true that if we say good-bye to the language, we shall be left with no tool with which we can and do succeed in communication. But it does not mean that it is the best tool. Our present language is so undeveloped that we shall be never in a position to describe the things under consideration meaningfully. So in such a situation what we are expected to do is the more careful use of such a defective linguistic tool. Our wielding of this linguistic tool in a careless manner will never succeed in describing the genuinely real things as they are; but, rather, it will philosophically ruin us. Therefore, Nāgārjuna makes us understand that *Śūnyatā* functions primarily as a censor of proliferative, unjustifiable and untenable platonism.[62] Its logical and methodological considerations neither separately nor conjunctively go to show that what is intended to convey by *Śūnyatā* is utter voidity[63] as it is many times pointed out. In its negative aspect the notion, rather, is employed mainly to do away the two extreme philosophical positions—nihilism and realism and to pave a way to the Buddha's philosophical position—which later on Nāgārjuna puts forth as his philosophical position—viz. *Madhyamā Pratipad*—a middle between two extreme poles. For, the former of the two above-mentioned positions holds that nothing exists while the latter holds that everything that we take to be real exists. Likewise, in epistemology there are corresponding two extreme positions : nothing can be known ond no knowledge claim can be justified. On the level of logic and methodology, again, it is held that the language which we normally and commonsensically use correctly describes the nature of things genuinely given to us, the concepts and categories it brings forth are enormously important in explaining the nature of such things structurally and constitutionally, while the counterpart of such a position holds that no language whatever, no conceptual and categorical frame whatever, is or can be available to us that is philosophically illuminating and intellectually rewarding. But when it comes to the consideration of those and only those things which a rightly understood *Pratītyasamutpāda*, as the Buddha intended to put it forth, is supposed to make available to us and correctly characterising their nature structurally and constitutionally, none of these positions can be our guide. Instead, we land into insurmountable confusion and error. Given such confusion, error, misunderstanding and conceptual bewilderment with which the proper import of Buddha's philosophical teaching was attempted to be brought out, Nāgārjuna took it to be his philosophic duty and intellectual responsibility to clear this kind of fog of misunderstanding with a view to bring out that sort of import and significance of *Pratītya Samutpāda* that is different from its commonsensical understanding and presented the philosophic position of the Buddha in a proper way. It is for this purpose that, as we saw, he employs and exploits the methodological tool of *Sūnyatā* with both of its aspects—positive to defend the understanding of *Pratītyasamutpāda* which was intended by the Buddha, and negative to clear away the fog of misunderstanding, distortion and abberation that were attempted to be smuggled into his philosophic teaching to make a coricature of it.

Thus, *Sūnyatā* at the hands of Nāgārjuna is designed in such a way that with the help of it one can weed through such philosophical positions which are either distortions of the philosophical position of the Buddha or are at least at variance from it and come to grasp *Tattva*—that which is the case.[64] By the employment of *Sūnyatā*, Nāgārjuna did not want to annihilate that which is rightfully and legitimately there. 'It is rather an occam's razor used by a nominalist to shave of Plato's beard. It is a bulldozer operated to crush away that sort of ontological slum that is generated out of linguistic traps, conceptual puzzlement and categorial cobwebs'.[65] *Sūnyatā* is a device with the help of which *Paramārthasatya* is sought to be segregated from *lokasaṁvṛttisatya*.[66] *Sūnyatā* is, thus, neither a total doing away of the things and making the world void nor is it a hold-all that can accommodate any number and kind of items under the sun.[67] It is rather a powerful purgative prescribed to those who are suffering from indigestion of philosophic ideas, a powerful methodological weapon with the help of proper wielding of which one is expected to develop such a philosophical position which could be said to be the one the Buddha endeavour to put before us. But one will not be able to comprehend such a position as well as understood the principal points in which it differed from the then currently held philosophical positions unless one gets to know the focus and perspective from which it was developed. Such a persprctive, as we shall argue in the next chapter, is *Nirvāṇa*, which in its

-turn is instrumental in fashioning out the intended correct philosophical position—*Madeyamā Pratipad*. We saw in this chapter, that at the hands of Nāgārjuna rightly understood *Pratītyasamutpāda* and properly employed *Sūnyatā* are very intimately connected with each other. The philosophical position called *Madhyamā Pratipad* is very-intimately connected with *Nirvāṇa*—the perspective. But the perspective under consideration is very closely connected with *Pratītyasamutpāda* and *Sūnyatā*. Hence merely on the basis of understanding *Pratītya-samutpāda* or *Sūnyata* separately, as also merely on the basis of grasping interrelationship between them is not both necessary and sufficient to be able to understand the full and proper significance of the philosophical position - *Madhyamā Pratipad*. To come to that has to be mediated through our coming to outline and understand the perspective - *Nirvāṇa*, which is connected with *Pratītyasamutpāda* and *Sūnyatā* on the one hand and *Madhymā Pratipad* - the philosophic position, on the other. It is, therefore, to the task of explaining the nature of *Nirvāṇa* and bringing out its importance in Nāgārjuna's philosophy that we turn in the next chapter.

NOTES

1. *Madhyamakaśāstra*; 24.18
   Yaḥ Pratītyasamutpādaḥ śūnyatāṁ tāṁ pracakṣmahe/
   Sā prajñaptirupādāya pratipatsaiva madhpamā//

2. Marathe, M.P., "Nāgārjuna and Candrakīrti on Śūnyatā;" (IPQ) Vol. VII, No. 4, p. 531.

3. Ibid, p. 531.

4. *Prasannapadā*, Iha hi śūnyatānāmeti sarvadharmāṇāṁ sāmānyalakṣaṇam iti abhyupagamāt, p. 107.

5. Ibid, mṛṣāsvabhāvānām padārthānāṁ/p. 5.
   laukikapadārthā nirupapattikā p. 72.

6. Ibid, Tathā mṛṣāsvabhāva api bhāvā p. 15.
   Madhyamakaśāstra 1.12
   Bhāvānāṁ niḥsvabhāvānāṁ na sattā vidyate yataḥ/

7. Ibid, 13.8 and Prasannapadā on it.

8. Murti, T.R.V., *The Central Philosophy of Buddhism* pp. 140-42
   The author suggests that by *Śūnyatā* Nāgārjuna is intended to mean the highest transce state of intellect which devices all dogmatic assertions and thereby reaches transcendental illumination.

9. Narain, Harsh, Śūnyavāda : Reinterpretation PEW Vol. 13 No. 4, pp. 311-338.
   The author at the very outset declares that the aim of writing this article is to restore the nihilistic character of *Śūnyavāda* of *Mādhyamikas* by throwing light on its so-called monistic as well as absolutistic character i.e. it was a refutation of Stcherbatsky and Stcherbatskians.

10. *Madhyamakaśāstra*; 24.1
    Yadi śūnyamidaṁ sarvamudayo nāsti na vyayah/
    caturṇāmāryasatyānāmabhāvaste prasajyate//

11. *Prasandapadā*; Sarvamidaṁ bāhyamādhyātmikaṁ.../p. 209.

12. *Madhyamakaśāstra*; 24.6
    Śūnyatām phalasadbhāvamadharmaṁ dharmamevaca/
    sarvasaṁvyavahārāṁśca laukikān pratibādhase//

13. Ibid, 24.7
    Atra brūmaḥ śūnyatāyāṁ na tvaṁ vetsi prayojanaṁ
    Śūnyatāṁ śūnyatārthaṁ ca tata evaṁ vihanyase//

14. *Prasannapada*; Sa bhavān svavikalpanayaiva nāstitvaṁ śūnyatārtha.../p. 214.

15. *Ibid*, Evaṁ pratītyasamutpādaśabdasya yo'rthaḥ sa eva śūnyatāśabdasyārthaḥ......niyataṁ vihanyase/p. 214.

16. *Ibid*, Na ca vayaṁ abhāvārthaṁ śūnyatārthaṁ vyācakṣmahe ......śūnyatādarśanadūṣaṇaṁ/p. 217.

17. *Ibid*, Śūnyāḥ sarvadharmā niḥsvabhāvayogena/p. 122.

18. *Ibid*, Yadi saṁsāro nāma kaścit syāt, niyataṁ tasya pūrvaṁ api syāt, paścimaṁ api......./p. 95.

19. *Ibid*, Syāt ātmā, yadā samsāra eva syāt.../p. 95.

20. *Ibid*, Syāt ātmā yadi duḥkhameva syāt/p. 100.

21, *Ibid*, "......tasmāt nāsti samsāraḥ"/p. 95.
   "......tasmāt svabhāvato na santi duḥkhādīni"/p. 102.
   "......samsārābhāvācca na asti ātmā iti"/p. 96.

22. *Ibid*, Yadi karma nāma kincit syāt pratyayasamutpannam vā bhavet apratyayasamutpannam vā ? p. 141.

23. *Prasannapadā*, Sarvecamoṣadharmāṇaḥ samskārāḥ...... mṛṣābhavanti/p. 104.

24. *Ibid*, Syādetadevam, yadi samsarga...na tvasti/p. 110.

25. *Ibid*, yastu akṛtakaḥ sa svabhāvaḥ/p. 114.

26. *Ibid*, yattu yasya parāyattam na tattasyātmīyam/p. 115.

27. *Ibid*, Ko'yam svabhāvaḥ?......sarvathānutpāda eva.../p. 116.

28. *Ibid*, Syāt kālatrayaprajñaptiheturbhāvasvabhāvaḥ............ bhavet/p. 163.

29. *Ibid*, Yataśca evam vicāraṇe kālatrayam nāsti,......./p. 164.

30. *Madhyamakaśāstra*, Chapter No. 14.

31. *Ibid*, Chapter No. 21.

32. *Ibid*, Chapter No. 20.

33. *Ibid*, Chapter No. 22.

34. *Ibid*, Chapter No. 23.

35. *Madhyamakaśāstra*, 24.18
   Yaḥ pratītyasamutpādaḥ śūnyatām tām pracakṣmahe sā prajñaptirupādāya pratipatsaiva madhyamā/

36. *Prasannapadā*; Samśayamithyājñānāpākaraṇārtham......idam śāstramārabdhavān/p. 13.

37. *Ibid*, Na khalu āryāḥ...tathaiva lokam bodhayanti/p. 19.

38. *Ibid*, Naiva hi vayam sarvapramāṇa prameyavyavahāram satyamity ācakṣmahe kintu vyavasthapyata....../p. 23.

39 *Ibid*, vastusvarūpeṇa avidyamānasyaiva te nāstitvaṁ pratipannāḥ/p. 157.

40. *Ibid*, yathāvadviditavastusvarūpāṇām mādhyamikanāṁ/p. 157.

41. *Madhyamakaśāstra*; 24.6
Sarvasanivyavahārāṅśea laukikān pratibādhase/

42. *Ibid*, Śūnyamiti navaktavyaṁ aśūnyaṁ yadi vā bhavet/22.11.

43. *Prasannapadā*; Iha sarveṣāṁ eva dṛṣṭikṛtānāṁ sarvagraha abhiniveśānām yannisaraṇam apravṛttiḥ sā śūnyatā/p. 108.

44. Marathe, M P., "Nāgārjuna and Candrakīrti on Śūnyatā" (IPQ) Vol. VII, No. 4, p. 533.

45. *Ibid*, p. 533.

46. *Ibid*, p. 534.

47. *Ibid*, p, 535.

48. *Ibid*, p. 535.

49. *Prasannapadā*, Dharmaśabdo'yaṁ................
svalakṣaṇadhāraṇārthena........./p. 132.

50. *Ibid*,......tathāgatena niḥsvabhāvatvaṁ eva sarvadharmāṇāṁ spaṣṭamāveditaṁ/p. 65.

51. *Ibid*, śūnyāḥ sarvadharmā niḥsvabhāvayogena/p. 193.

52. Marthe, M.P.; "Nāgārjuna and Candrakīrti on Śūnyatā" IPQ, Vol. VII No. 4, p. 536.

53. *Prasannapadā*: Yadāca aśūnyāḥ padārthā na santi...p. 107.

54. *Ibid*, Yadā tu padārthameva kancinna paśyāmaḥ...p. 104.

55. *Ibid*, Sapekṣāṇāṁ api padārthānām sasvābhāvyadarśanāt p. 86.

56. *Ibid*, Tadyathā kulaputra māyākāranātake......
yantrakārakāritā yantrayuvatḥ....../p. 15.

57. *Ibid*, bhavānāṁ ca pratītyasamutpannatvāt/p. 30.

58. *Ibid*, Yataśca evaṁ kṛtrimasya parasāpekṣaya ca svabhāvat-vaṁ neṣṭaṁ/p. 115.

59. *Ibid*,...na santi sarvabhāvāḥ/p. 120.

60. *Ibid*, na vidyate sattā svabhāvaḥ sarvabhāvānāṁ.../p. 122.

61. Marathe, M.P., "Nāgārjuna and Candrakīrti on Śūnyatā (IPQ), Vol. VII No. 4, p. 537.

62. *Ibid*, p. 538.

63. *Ibid*, p. 538.

64. *Madhyakaśāstra* 18.9
Aparapratyayaṁ śāntaṁ prapañcairaprapañcitaṁ /
Nirvikalpamanānārthametattatvasya lakṣaṇam //

65. Marathe, M.P., "Nāgārjuna and Candrakīrti on Śūnyatā" IPQ, Vol. VII No. 4, p. 538.

66. *Ibid*, p. 538.

67. *Ibid*, p. 538.

CHAPTER IV

NIRVĀṆA

In the second and third chapters we discussed the doctrine of *Paratītya Samutpāda* and the notion of *Śūnyata* respectively. We, there, proposed what seems to us to be their proper import. The doctrine of *Pratītya Samutpāda*, we argued, is the thesis about the nature of the world and the connected things in it.[1] It therefore, stands for an ontological model explaining the nature of the world and the things in it. The things in the world, as we pointed out, are according to Nagarjuna, discrete particular entities. They are given to us successively or conjunctively. The only smallest common denominator of both these phenomena is that things are connected. The doctrine further tells us that when things are presented in succession we get sequence. But merely given sequence or succession we cannot hope to maintain that continuity is the structural feature of the world. For, the former is not both the necessary and sufficient condition of continuity. Things in the flow are merely connected with the one another and in consequences do give us a kind of chain, though it is not necessarily a causal one, since every causal chain is a chain but not the converse. Hence, just the fact of things, being connected should not be used for their causal connectedness. Thus, proper understanding of the doctrine of *Pratītya Samutpāda* means to acknowledge that things in the world, given in an uninterrupted flow of them, are discrete, unique and particular and are presented to us one after the other. Continuity, which generally we are accustomed to count as a structural feature of the world, could in fact, at the most, be said to be the resultant feature of it, where the so-called knower has a large, if not total part to contribute.

In the chapter on *Śūnyata* we pointed out that *Śūnayata* is a methodological tool used by the Buddha covertly but exploited and articulated by Nāgārjuna quite overtly. Proper understanding of the nature of the things presented in succession and thereby forming a flow (of things) amounts to the comprehension that they are discrete, unique particulars and yet connected things such that no two of them are identical with each other nor is one so similar to another that both of them could be referred to by one and the same referential expression. With a view to bring out such a feature of things as given to us and also to make us aware of some of the fundamental inadequacies of the kind of language we are accustomed to employ in our common mode of communication, the concept of *Śūnyatā* appears basically to be employed to bring home to us three main points : (i) The language which we generally use to talk about things discorts rather than reveals their appropriate nature (ii) It is a mistake of a very fundamental kind to confuse between properties of possession and properties of attribution. And, (iii) It is invain to hold that, that the kind of world and things inhabiting it is the factual world which best matches with our expectations, hopes, aspiration and the kind of language we are accustomed use no matter how much at varience such a world and things belonging to it turn out to be from what as a matter of fact they are.

Thus, while *Pratītya Samutpāda* is an attempt at proper understanding the nature of things and the world, *Śūnyatā* is a methodological tool not only wielded to put forth and defend a basically nominalistic framework[2] but is also directed at exposing some of some of the major pit-falls, errors and confusions we harbour but which, on closer analysis, turn out to be just children of our brain, some of the prominent of which are : (a) that every property things is thought to be possessing is taken to be real, and hence structurally connected with it. (b) that generality which is indicative of shareability is basic feature of things; (c) that everything that we are prone to hold to be real is existent as a matter of fact no matter how long it allows Plato to grow his beard and (d) that epistemological objects, one and all, are as real as things properly belonging to the world. There is certainly a connection between *Pratītya Samutpāda* and *Śūnyatā* not only because the latter is a procalmation of non-obtainability and hence unreality of all inessential things, their believed to be permanent features,[3] their independent existence, or non-constitutivity of all states[4] but also because it advocates slicing off of all illegitimate viewings,[5] upholds unreality of all properties of attribution[6] as also because through wilding of such a methodological tool we come to obtain an illumination that much of what is considered to constitute the furniture of platonistically real world is not ontologically so and thus we are led, rightly, to hold that the only world that has a genuine outological status is the one that is given to us through the spectum of properly understood *Pratītya Samutpāda*. Thus, as stated earlier, a close connection between the two is discernible.[7] Something of this kind is not. even methodologically, unnatural to turn about. For, while the former intends to bring to our notice things and the world as they are structured and constituted, the latter amounts to tell us how a thing and a world should not be considered to be structured or constituted. though ordinarily and unwittingly we take them to be so. Thus, however, indirectly and implicitly it might be, it is obvious and natural that they converge upon each other.[8] Furthermore, we are also told and we hope to explain it in the sequel that both *Pratītya Samutpāda* as well as *Śūnyatā* are jointly and severally connected with *Nirvāṇa*. Accordingly, one cannot hope to gain an insight into Nāgārjuna's explanation of *Nirvāṇa* without diving deep into its connection with *Pratītya Samutpāda* on the one hand and with *Śūnyatā* on the other. Hence. our understanding of the connection between *Pratītya Samupāda* and *Śūnyatā* is preparing the necessary intellectual make up for our proper understanding of Nāgārjuna's treatment to *Nirvāṇa*. This is especially so because his explantion of *Nirvāṇa*, as will be shown in the sequel, is very importantly connected with that of *Saṃsāra*, which in turn is inseverable from a platonic world-view which is wrongly believed to be an outcome of *Pratītya Samutpāda*. But the connection of *Nirvāṇa* with *Śūnyatā*, too, cannot be overlooked.[9] This again is not something inscrutable to understand. For, if *Pratītya Samutpāda* is shown to be connected with *Nirvāṇa* then *Śūnyatā* must also stand connected with it, because as pointed above, they are connected with each other. Such a feature of *Nirvāṇa* does not arise merely out of the prima facie contingent fact of three being closely connected with one another but also because, we are told these expressions are synonymous with one another.[10] Thus, the three pillars of Nāgārjuna's philosophy viz.—*Pratītya Samutpāda*, *Śūnyāta* and *Nirvāṇa* are so intrinsically and intimately connected that an explanation of any one of them just cannot be given independently of the other two. Hence, it is simply unavoidable that any one of them cannot be

isolated from the rest two. Not to have properly understood this
and its implications appears to be one of the major shortcomings
of the majority of the attempts made in this direction.[11]

Accordingly, therefore, first we come to take a brief critical
review of some of the main attempts of the so-called proper
explanation of *Nirvāṇa* as it is said to be intended by pre-Nāgārjuna
scholars as well as Nāgārjuna. Later on we turn to our exposition
of it as Nāgārjuna intends to understand it in the light of the above
mentioned crucially important problems viz. it connection with
Pratītya Samutpāda, Śūnyatā on the one hand and its place within
the philosophic position of Nāgārjuna viz. *Madhyamā Pratipad* on
the other. Some of the latter kind of connection will indeed be in
anticipation of the treatment of *Madhyamā Pratipad* to be undertaken in the last chapter. But something of this kind is at least
partly, excusable for two reasons : (i) the concept of Nivāṇa in
Nāgārjuna's philosophy cannot satisfactorily be discussed in
isolation from his philosophic position and (ii) Such an anticipatory
treatment, we hope and believe, will make a smooth transition from
this to the next chapter. So coming then, to the treatment of
Nirvāṇa as Nāgārjuna understood it at the hands of previous
scholars

Historical Background of Nirvāṇa

Before we take this task in hand it is neeessary to take a
glance at the circumstances in which Nāgārjuna was required to
undertake the exercise of re-presentation and reformulation of the
import of Buddha's philosophieal teaehing. For, Nāgārjuna came,
unfortunately, to be misunderstood at the hands of posterity on
two principal counts :

(a) misunderstanding about the circumstances that necessiated
Nāgārjuna to undertake the intellectual exercise that he undertook
and (b) misunderstanding about his philosophical position alongwith distortion of his explanation of *Pratītya Samutpāda, Śūnyatā*
and/or *Nirvāṇa*. It is often held that Nāgārjuna might have come to
be misunderstood only on the latter count. This, however, is a
partial truth. These two kinds of misunderstandings about
Nāgārjuna, again, are so connected with each other that one cannot hope to make sense of and lay it bare without undertaking
similar exercise with regard to the other. It is further important

to understand that this kind of double misunderstanding about Nāgārjuna is not something to which accidental or oriental scholars alone have fallen prey. As truth has no geographical boundaries so too an error and confusion. This is noticeable in the case under consideration as well. To bring this point home in clearer relief, therefore, we first probe into the circumstances that led Nāgārjuna to philosophize at all.

After the demise of the Buddha a problem as to what is the teaching of the Buddha—both religious and philosophical—surfaced and occupied people's attention over quite a long period of time. The problem became crucial especially because the Buddha did not commit anything to writing.[12] Of these, the problem of the religious teaching of the Buddha was considerably taken care of by the Councils which come to be appointed in succession. But the problem of his philosophical teaching continued to bother interested persons. On this count various attempts must have come to be made some of which fortunately have been available to us in the form of Canonical literature. *Niāvāṇa* is one of the important topics in Buddha's philosophical teaching. Hence the problem as to what did the Buddha mean by *Nirvāṇa*, too become a hotly discussed and debated among them. But in the Canonical literature as also prior to Nāgārjuna a systematic attempt to present Buddha's philosophic teaching does not seem to have been made. Nāgārjuna undertook to make such an attempt. Since in the philosophic teaching of the Buddha *Pratītya Samutpāda*, *Śūnyata* and *Nirvāṇa* occupy a vital role it is no wonder that Nāgārjuna made serious attempt to systematize Buddha's philosophic perspective about them. But if we glance through the canonical literature, we find that various attempts were made to interpret *Nirvāṇa* prior to Nāgārjuna. There are frequent direct mentions of what in plain language, is called 'thirst extinction' where *Nibbāna* is taken to be nothing else but deliverance—deliverance from desire, hate and delusion.[13] For. desire, hate, delusion etc. represent thirst of one's craving. Therefore, it is extinction of thirst (*Tanhākkhayo*).[14] Sometimes scholars took *Nibbāna* to be the highest bliss.[15] From the dialogues of the king Milind and venerable Nāgasena it appears that (after deliverance of the Buddha) *Nirvāṇa* came to signify summum bonum of Man.[16] Though the word was primarily taken to mean in the negative sense as 'cessation' or 'absence of something' yet later on a positive significance came to be attached to it.[17] Thus in the pre-Nāgārjuna time early Buddhist scholars consistently hold *Nirvāṇa* to be something positive. It is such an incorrect interpretation which must have necessitated Nāgārjuna to put fotrh a proper interpretation of it. Here it would not be altogether out of context, to outline, though in a sketchy way, by way of conjecture, the reasons that might have led the people to put forth such varient interpretation of *Nirvāṇa* in the pre-Nāgār-juna period. First, as pointed out above, the Buddha did not commit anything to writing; and prior to Nāgārjuna there was hardly any serious attempt to outline Buddha's philosophical doctrines. Similarly, after the passing away of the Buddha the Councils were formed and codifications of Buddha's religious teaching was made to guide people in their everyday mode of actions, faith and fellowship. It might also be the case that to give philosophical basis to such codification certain views were marshalled according to the intellectual richness of the advancing persons. Further, in the absence of any specific and articulated statement available in the written form it must have been exceedingly difficnlt to formulate his teaching on this count. As the time gap between the demise of the Buddha and such formulations went on increasing, inspite of considerable amount of head scratching and nut chewing, there must have surfaced considerable such attempts suitable to the then prevalent intellec-tual climats[18] and philosophical convenience of the scholars indulging in such exercises. In such a situation many persons and groups might have made heroic attempts to give a sketch of what the Buddha might have meant by *Nirvāṇa*. But in the absence of any serious philosophic consideration and proper methodological orientation attempts of this kind gave rise to bewildering variety of interpretations, each one claiming to be authentic and therefore superior to the rest of them. There, out of this situation must have arisen two problems : (a) which is the proper understanding of *Nirvāṇa* as the Buddha endeavoured to put forth and (b) in the face of such a variety of views, which one of them is to be taken to be more reliable, being consitsent with the Buddha's focus and perspective. It is here that lies the importance of Nāgārjuna as perhaps one of the first persons to present Buddha's philosophic teaching in a systematic and proper way. Secondly, the Buddha's major concern appears to be to undertake an intellectual hysterectomy of the womb that is germinative of that kind of platonism where everything comes to be given an ontological status no matter whether it is an object of expectation, emotion, will, desire and what not. Through our unwitting conferment of ontological status on them the world that we come to accept to be real is too unwieldy and it is well nigh impossible to seek to establish any philosophically interesting and methodologically desirable order in it. On this background Buddha's attempt to establish philosophy on firm foundation itself come to be twisted and his philosophy come to be religionized, psychologised and misleading epistemological perspective come to be linked up with it. This had to be undone and Buddha's philosophy in its proper import and significance had to be presented to save the posteriority from falling into further confusion and error. It is here that the importance of Nāgārjuna lies. He is critical not only of bad philosophy done by non-Buddhists but also by Buddhist themselves and more so of the latter kind because it is that which is more prone to present a distorted picture of Buddha's philosophic perspective.[19] For example, (a) Taking *Nirvāṇa* as an ethico-religious ideal become the basis of reconsidering worldly transactions. As a result it comes to be argued that each and every activity ought to be considered in terms of its moral and religious acceptability. (b) Taking that *Nirvāṇa* consists in freeing an individual from worldly miseries[20] and saying that it helps the self to migrate from this world to another world[21] leads to (i) under-rating the world in which we live and (ii) the fallacy of duplication of the world. (c) Taking *Nirvāṇa* as permanent release from worldly misries like hatred, pain and delusion etc. and on eternal rest of the self from the cycle of birth and death[22] implies (i) that there is a self (which is again on Buddha's view a misnomer), (ii) that it can be permanently released from worldly affairs (iii) that it is immortal and (iv) that it can migrate from this miserable world to another— perhaps perfect and ideal world. (d) Taking *Nirvāṇa* as an ethico-religious ideal leads to the situation that an individual pays least attention to the worldly transaction and refuses to understand the nature of the world. As a result of this such a person ultimately remains philosophically ignorant about it. (e) It is held that in order to attain *Nirvāṇa* one is required to go through a long and ardous path of self mortification. Over and above all these points such an interpretation of *Nirvāṇa* fails to understand unreality of unreal objects which are created out of human efforts on mental and/or linguistic level. But considering *Nirvāṇā* as an ideal also fails to account for its philosophical significance, as there is no systematic attempt of philosophical investigation behind it. It is this situation, indeed frustrating one, that made Nāgārjuna to repudiate conventional meaning of some of the Buddhistic terms in order to enable people to see some of the grave mistakes that they are likely to embrace about Buddha's thought. Therefore, Nāgārjuna says that *Nirvāṇa* is not something social, psychological, ontological or even religious for that matter. It is rather a perspective that one needs to develop in order to understand the unreality of unreal objects which layman considers as if existent in his crude way of thinking. *Nirvāṇa* as a philosophical focus has, indeed, bearings upon social moral, psychological, ontological or epistemological considerations. But, nevertheless, it does not and cannot make *Nirvāṇa* itself ontological, social or religious for that matter.

One may raise a question at this juncture that why should it be considered as a focus or perspective by totally deviating from the pre-Nāgārjuna interpretation of it ? To this we answer that taking *Nirvāṇa* as a proper perspective or a (philosophical) focus alone fits to the preaching of the Buddha and thereby into the entire framework of Nāgārjuna's philosophy. For (i) we are generally prone to consider the nature of the world by taking into consideration a particular aspect of it. It being partial in nature leads to the fallacy of commission or omission. Therefore, it is an attack on aspectival approach about the world. (ii) Our assumption that such a partial perspective (*dṛṣṭi*) alone is true leads us to embrace dogmatic position which in its turn fails to represent the nature of the world as it is. It is, therefore, an attack on the dogmatic approach, too, about the world. (iii) *Nirvāṇa* is not any goal or ideal either to be charished or accomplished, because if such a goal is to be cherished, it will not have any fundamental concern with philosopoical investigations and the whole mission of philosophization would turn out to be insignificant. Therefore, it is an attack on teleological or futuristic approach about the human behavior. (iv) We may perhaps equate *Nirvāṇa* with ontological or epistemological spheres. It may thus present a particular view of the world or human knowledge but in that case our investigation will be limited to one or the other domain of inquiry. Since it is not expected of *Nirvāṇa* it is an attack on domain-wise de-limitations.

There are two perspectives of looking at the world. They are :

(a) *Lokasamvṛtti or vyavahāra* and (b) *Paramārtha*, and we shall have an occasion to turn to their consideration in greater detail in the sequel. For the present, however, it suffices to note that these two perspectives naturally pre-suppose corresponding two pictures of the world. If these two pictures of the world are, at all, to be compared and contrasted it can be done through a focus which will throw light on both the pictures of the world and will show that what is there as a matter of fact and what is not there. It is this philosophical focus—*Nirvāṇa* which enables us to develop a philosophic understanding of the nature of the world and the things in it. Therefore, when such a proper perspective shall come to bear upon the problems and issues of above mentioned domains of inquiry, we are more likely to get profound insight into them such that some of our most cherished views would turn out to be untenable and would, in consequence, have to be discarded. Thus *Nirvāṇa* as a focus is a torch-bearer in our philosophic scrutiny and is not a matter of luxury in speculation ; it is rather a necessary pre-condition of an honest intellectual investigation. Such an investigation must tell us not that everything that we take to be real is real but rather taking what things to be real would be warrantable, philosophically interesting and intellectually illuminating and at the same time enable us to weed through the otherwise thick forest of misunderstanding, errors and confusion. Therefore according to Nāgārjuna *Nirvāṇa* consists in 'proper understanding' or developing a proper perspective and cannot be considered even in imagination that it is an end of life or getting away from worldly transaction. It is but a direction to the discovery of the way things truly are.[23]

Pūrvapakṣin of Nāgārjuna says that if everything is (*Śūnya*) devoid of self existence, *Nirvāṇa* turns out to be meaningless.[24] To this Nāgārjuna replies that this would be true if *Śūnayātā* is taken in its literal sense of emptiness. But it should not be understood in its literal sense of emptiness. Rather it should be used as a methodological tool to do away with the otherwise proliferative ontology, misleading epistemological weed and erroneous linguistic considerations arising out of misunderstanding on various levels. So the contention under consideration cannot be upheld. Consequently, *Nirvāṇa* does not turn out to be meaningless but remains philosophically rich, provided one understands it in the proper spirit. In *Nirvāṇa* there is certainly a shift—a shift of perspective or a focus. But this by no means indicates a passage from one life to another, nor from the world we are generally familiar with to any other world. The change of perspective under consideration is so crucial that it may be linked with a passage—passage from ignorance to knowledge, from confusion to clarity. It is of profound importance because in the light of it many items, doctrines and principles which otherwise happen to be considered to be philosophically rewarding turn out to be spurious and ill-founded on closer scrutiny.

But inspite of such a kind of exposition of *Nirvāṇa* at the hands of Nāgārjuna and further clarifiactions of it in the *Prasannapadā* by Chandrakīrti, in the post Nāgārjuna period, the critics of Buddhist philosophy of western origin, who studied early Buddhist literature and are considered to be an authority on Buddhist philosophy, come to uphold the view that *Nirvāṇa* is an ethical ideal.[25] Some of them believed that *Nirvāṇa* is the happiness after death. In the same vein. Prof. A.B. Keith[26] Paul Dahlke[27] expressed the view that *Nirvāṇa* is the summum bonum. Scholars of Indian origin like Dr. S.N. Dasgupta[28] or Dr. S. Radhakrishnan[29] also hold a similar view, following largely in the foot-steps of western scholars, that *Nirvāṇa* is the highest bliss. Not only that but some modern scholars strongly hold the view that Buddhist *Nirvāṇa* mighs have sprung from an influence of *Upaniṣadic* philosophy on the Buddha and as such it resembles with non-Buddhist concept of *Mokṣa*[30] *Apavarga*[31] or *Kaivalya*.

It is needless to say that all these views expressed by scholars and critics of Buddha's philosophy in post-Nāgārjuna era are far from the Nāgārjunian treatment to Buddha's philosophy is general and *Nirvāṇa* in particular.

This kind of situation is enough to provoke anybody to consider the problem of *Nirvāṇa* afresh and point out that Nāgārjuna, following the Buddha, takes *Nirvāṇa* as a philosophical solution to philosophical problems. It is neither an ethical nor a religious ideal, but is a proper perspective or a focus that one ought to adopt to be able to have a proper grasp of things in the world. We hope that this preliminary discussion is sufficient for being able to accomplish the purpose in the hand. Let us turn to two technical terms, which Nāgārjuna uses as a stepping stone in the comprehension of *Nirvāṇa* as a philosophical perspective.

Nāgārjuna on 'Lokasṁvṛtti, and 'Paramārtha Śatya'

These two expressions, as pointed out above, are employed by Nāgārjuna to represent two world perspectives one of common man and another of a philosopher, who has developed a profounder insight. *Lokasaṁvṛtti Satya* and *Paramārtha Satya* are instrumental for our comprehension of a proper perspective—*Nirvāṇa*. By *Lokasṁvṛtti* he means our everyday experience of the world—our normal veredical experience as well as illusory and hallucinatory experience. It includes fictitious things which are utterly non-existent like a ghost or sky-lotus or a son of a barren-woman.[32]

Such a *Lokasaṁvṛtti* also gives due room to social considerations such as good or bad action, fruit of action[33] etc. It is common pattern that without probing into the real status of all these we unhesitatingly admit all of them to be the part and parcel of the furniture of the world. Not only that but sometimes we take the activities involved in knowing process[34] also to be real as tables and chairs. For example, look at the position taken by the *Purvapakṣin*[35] of Nāgārjuna who supposes himself to be a common conjurer—the position, which of course, is strongly refuted by both Nāgārjuna and Candrakīrti. But the view upheld by him is significantly indicative of the common pattern of thinking and how the *laukika vyavahāras* are carried out. Such a *Lokasaṁvṛtti* when it is taken as the basis of our knowledge, it covers up entirely the real nature of the thing and makes them appear otherwise. Such a *Lokasaṁvṛtti* is not functioning merely in the realm of things, but it also covers the language-based transaction of things. It, Candrakīrti explains, is that where the nature of the things and/or entities is explained in terms of utter reciprocity and mutual dependence of them. It conceals or envelops the nature of things, entities and their dispositions. It is called *Lokavyavāhara* or the world of ordinary transaction.[36] In such an ordinary world an individual is busy in characterising things with the help of odd and easy going distinctions without probing into the nature of them and ultimately is bound to be deprived of proper perspective about the reality.

The fundamental distinguishing mark of this view of the world is not so much that it is held by laymen. It is also not that our ordinary modes of thought, action and fellowship are ordered in it. Rather its principal traits are : reiflcation, duplication, proliferation. In so far as it takes not only those things which are real to be real but also those which are not, it duplicates number of knowable entities. Conferring reality status on entities, relations, properties, dispositions as also upon what appears to be real, or even what is believed to be signified by our so-called significant expressions its process of reification and proliferation of things taken to be real grows unchecked. In such a world we not only fail to grasp what genuinely is real but are also at a loss to adopt any position that is philosophically interesting. Due to multiplication of entities far too beyond the warranted limit annihilates the very prospect of adopting a tenable world view, for through our coming to embrace category-mistakes, errors and confusions our conceptual geography turns topsy-turvy and in consequence the very possibility of coherent and consistent knowledge is removed from our intellectual sight. One thing, however, is clear and it is that it is this world that makes *saṁsāra* (passage from one world/life to another) possible and real.

When contrasted with *Lokasaṁvṛtti Satya, Paramārtha Satya* is said to be that where the *laukika* structure of thinking, behaviour etc. ceases to exist and an individual comes out of the modes of 'I' and 'mine'. In *Paramārtha Satya* there is no possibility of worldly transaction.[37] Candrakīrti describes *Paramārtha Satya* as that which is not of the nature of reification and duplication (*niṣprapañca*) and is free from hypostetization (*nirvikalpa*).[38] Therefore, there remains nothing for our ordinary language to refer to. When one comprehends this, such a state of affair can neither be conceived nor be made knowable to others through commonsensical conceptual framework.[39] For both require the use of ordinary language, and its conceptual ambiguity and imprecision thwarts the very possibility of capturing such a world and accordingly making use of it we cannot hopefully communicate nature, structure and constitution of such a world through such a language without distortion and bewitchments. When one realizes the futility of the present linguistic tool, he refrains[40] from making use of it. For, it is so inadequate and defective that it distorts rather to reveals the nature of uniquely particular things and the world constituted of them. Thus, *Paramārtha Satya* give us corresponding perspective about the world.

Now, these two world pictures, depending upon corresponding two world perspectives, when seen through the philosophical focus lead to the comprehension of that alone which is genuinely there and enables us to grasp that structure of the world as it has. *Nirvāṇa* is such a perspective. Thus, *Nirvāṇa* enables us to consider *Saṁvṛtti* as well as *Paramārtha* from a sort of equidistance. And taking *Paramārtha* as real picture of the world, when *Saṁvṛtti* is examined, much of the rubbish part of it goes away and the remnant becomes identical with *Paramārtha Satya*. Our understanding *Lokasaṁvṛtti* and *Paramārtha Satya* through the focus of *Nirvāṇa* throws light as to why does Nāgārjuna identify *Saṁsāra* with *Nirvāṇa* by saying that there is not the slightest difference between them[41] and whatever can be ascribed to *Saṁsāra* can also be ascribable to *Nirvāṇa*,[42] *Saṁsāra* and *Nirvāṇa* being two focuses adopted by a common man and a person having developed a profounder insight to look at the world. Both of them accept that there are certain things by their very nature and they exist in the world. But over and above this common man gathers an impression that objects of illusory and hallucinatory experience are also real. But the adoption of the focus of *Nirvāṇa* does away the unreality of such unreal objects and the things which are real in *Nirvāṇa* also turn out to be real in *saṁsāra* but not conversely. Thus intellectual cleanliness on the part of layman cleanses away the proliferative dirt of *saṁsāra* and the ontic range of such a cleansed world coincides with the ontic range of *Nirvāṇa* and thus they remain co-extensive.[43] This being the case, *Saṁsāra* and *Nirvāṇa* cannot be regarded as having related with one another in product-producer relation as pointed out by Nāgārjuna's opponent,[44] when he says that *Nirvāṇa* is real because *Saṁsāra* is real.

One may raise a question at this juncture that if *Paramārtha Satya* is truth properly so called, then why is one required to undergo the exercise of understanding the truth improper (*saṁvṛtti*) first and the truth proper afterwards?[45] The reason behind it is that we are born and nurtured in the atmosphere of *lokasaṁvṛtti*. We are naturally and obviously brought up into the atmosphere of *lokasaṁvṛtti*. So starting with what is familiar to us by way of common pattern of behaviour first enables us to understand the logic of common mode of behaviour, speech and thinking and through the development of proper perspective one is expected to slice off the dispensable part of that world that has been given rise to due to the *saṁvṛtti* leading to the comprehension of *Paramārtha Satya.* Thus, *Paramārtha Satya* is to be understood and discovered through removal of *Saṁvṛtti.* Our understanding *lokasaṁvṛtti Satya* and adoption of the proper perspective—*Nirvāṇa* takes us to understand the *Paramārtha Satya.* And unless we know properly *Paramārtha Satya* we cannot be said to have adopted a proper perspective correctly i.e. our understanding *niṣprapañca svabhāva* of *Paramārtha Satva*[46] is directly connected with our adoption of the perspective of *Nirvāṇa.* Nāgārjuna, in this connection, further contends that it is not the system envisaged by himself. Rather he is endeavouring to explain Buddha's philosophy which the Buddha himself comes to put forth,[47] which investigates into the domain of two different comprehensions of the world with a view to outline and sketch proper philosophic understanding and insight that one needs to develop. Thus, to explain the matter in a simple way he takes recourse to the two divergent comprehensions of the world not because he intends to defend and warrant both, but rather with a view to enlighten us as to which of them is philosophically interesting and intellectually illuminating. One who understands the problem and the solution in this way alone will be in a position to grasp Nāgārjuna's standpoint and thereby the philosophy of the Buddha. Failing to understand the connection between *Saṁvṛtti, Paramārtha Satya* and *Nirvāṇa,* one will come to accommodate everything i.e. factual, illusory, hallucinatory, social, religious, linguistic and what not as equally real.

Nirvāṇa : Non-Psychological and Non-Ontological

The development of proper perspective is necessary in order that we come to develop such an understanding of the world and things in it that is free from confusion, errors and misunderstanding so that it enables us to comprehend what lies at the heart of reality. But by contrast, such a focus should also enable us to understand anything that is unreal as unreal, for, otherwise, one is prone to take it as real. Adoption of such a focus has naturally repurcussions on ontological, epistemological or linguistic spheres and our explanation of the nature of the focus without taking a recourse to these fields may not help us either to modify or change or if necessary, to give up the views that are already cherished in normal course of explanation as a proper form of it. But the *Pūrvapakṣin* of Nāgārjuna, concentrating upon the common pattern of behaviour, is not satisfied with Nāgārjuna's analysis of *lokasaṁvṛtti* and *Paramārtha Satya* as two perspectives of 'viewing' at the world. Rather, relying upon the experience as it goes, he tries to capture the 'perspective' within the fold of some explanatory device. He argues that *Nirvāṇa* is a psychological state of affair. For, in *Nirvāṇa* self gets rid of worldly life, mental framework, egoness etc. Therein modes of 'I' and 'Mine' disappear; expectations, feelings, dispositions and desires come to an end. Therefore, that which helps the self to get free from all psychological states must itself be psychological. To this Nāgārjuna replies that this contention would have been sound provided what it presupposes as psychological were there. But mere taking for granted that self,[48] ego, mental framework,[49] dispositions, expectations, desires[50] etc. are there does not make them real in an ontological sense of the term. Likewise, to say that expectations etc. come to an end in *Nirvāṇa* is philosophically illuminating in no way. *Nirvāṇa* is not a den of lion where one sees merely footprints of ingoing items but none of returning from it. In fact such a type of explanation one attempts to put forth due to misunderstanding and mental fabrication, which on a closer look turns out to be *vikalpas*, that the Buddha, having critically examined them, declared as the product of illusory experience.[51] Therefore, anybody's understanding, keeping an eye on illusory experience that such (illusory) qualities come to an end in *Nirvāṇic* state is as good as to try to extinguish fire in the dream with water.[52] That is, as fire and water in the dream are non-obtainable, so too, the act of extinguishing the so called fire. Similarly, the self, the activities of self and the act of its being liberated in *Nirvāṇic* state are all non-obtainable.[53] This being the case *Nirvāṇa* cannot be considered as a psychological state.

This endeavour of Nāgārjuna of rejecting to have some psychological import to *Nirvāṇa* did not obstruct the *Pūrvapakṣin* in looking forward and understanding it ontologically. The opponent, intelligent enough, in order to deduce that 'there is *saṁsāra*[54] from "there is *Nirvāṇa*" argues that even if one is prepared to grant, for the sake of an argument, that 'there is *Nirvāṇa*' yet this seems to run into rough water. For, as it is said that there is *Nirvāṇa* so too it is held (by ordinary persons) that there is *Saṁsāra*. It is further held that the two are *Pratidvandvi* of eace other. Now, since *Nirvāṇa* is *Pratidvandvi* of *Saṁsāra* why not grant that '*Saṁsāra* is there' ?   Though the argument of the *Pūrvapakṣin* appears, at least *prima facie*, to be well formulated and appealing, yet on closer scrutiny it turns out to be beset with many difficulties. Nāgārjuna's reply to this argument is two fold : (i) First, 'Nirvāṇa is there' is not a matter of convenience of anybody. As a focus it is genuine and real. But it does not mean that it is ontologically existent.   Hence, opponent's contention that ontological existence of *samsāra* is deducible from *Nirvāṇa* or vice versa is not acceptable.   For, the opponent deduces something that is ontological from that which is not ontological.   The focus under consideration, further, viz. *Nirvāṇa,* does enable us to consider ontological, epistemological or even methodological questions in a way different from the way they happen generally to be considered.   But this cannot be the basis of our saying that since the focus has ontological or epistemological aspect it, therefore, itself is ontological or epistemological.   Such a philosophical focus is a necessary pre-requisite of a proper philo- sophical understanding.   But this by no means makes the under- standing or the focus that makes its advent possible themselves ontological.   To subscribe to such a view is to make the misunder- standing that we normally already cherish worse confounded.   (ii) Nāgārjuna further contends that would it be neeessary and philosophically warrantable to take the simultaneous obtainability of *Samsāra* and *Nirvāṇa* in the scheme of our explanation ? i.e. does not our taking them to be simultaneously satisfiable lead to undesir- able consequence that we come to embrace a precarious position in philosophy ? For, if *Samsāra* and *Nirvāṇa* are two such divergent focuses of considering the world, which, being dismetrically opposed to each other, cannot be said to be simultaneously satisfiable than to say that they are and to hold that adopting any one of them is philosophically equally interesting and also satisfactory makes nonsense of one's coming to develop latter kind of focus at all. Further, it is equally untenable to hold that whichever focus we adopt the same world with the same kind of nature, structure and constitution of it would be available to us and hence which of these two focuses we chose is afterall immaterial. This is the mistake of a very fundamental kind that we are normally remain under the spell of. There is, thus, no way to conclude that because former is therefore the latter is or vice-versa.

Besides these two points, in saying that *Samsāra* is *Pratidvandvi* of *Nirvāṇa,* Nāgārjuna appears to endeavour to bring out another mistake in *Pūrvapakṣin's* argument. One of the basic assumption of the *Pūrvapakṣin* seems to be that *Pratidvandvitā* is a relation—a diadic relation for that matter, and no relation would be respectable unless it relates the reals. Now, given that *Nirvāna* is real or *Saṁsāra* is real and given further that they are related with each other by the relation of *Pratidvandvitā*' it is but natural to conclude that the other relatum too is real. But in coming to put forward such an argument the *Pūrvapakṣin* of Nāgārjuna seems to have confused relate of relation with reals and vice versa. A relation does require relata; but there is no one—one correspondence between relata and reals. In a reflexive relation for example, there certainly are two relata; but this does not imply that there are two things between which the reflexive relation under consideration is a relation. For, our being able to say that between *Saṁsāra* and *Nirvāna* there is a relation of *Pratidvandvitā*, it is sufficient to take them to be relate and it is not necessary to take them to be two things as well. Likewise, the *Pūrvapakṣin* seems to be misled by plurality of relata and plurality of things. Thus, without realizing simultaneous non-obtainability and non-satisfiability both of *Saṁsāra* and *Nirvāna*, he comes to defend his position on the basis of misunderstanding and confusion. Candrakīrti describes such an argument of *Pūrvapakṣin* with the help of a logical anology of such examples as 'not knowing the odour of sky-lotus',[55] or the meaninglessness of the questions such as 'whether a daughter of a barren woman is beautiful or not.'[56] Thus, here also Nāgārjuna rightly rejects the contention that *Saṁsāra* and *Nirvāna* are ontologically there as it involves a grave mistake of deducing ontology from something that is non-ontological, and hence is not acceptable.[57]

Nonetheless, *Purvapakṣin* of Nāgārjuna reiterates that *Nivāna* is ontological. For, it is *bhāvarūpa*.[58] Nāgārjuna immediately gets a clue of the force of the *Pūrvapakṣin's* argument. Suspecting that the *Pūrvapakṣin* may be drawing upon the opinion of some well-known thinkers like jaimini, Kaṇāda, Kapil etc.[59] and closely examining the argument under consideration refutes in detail the four possibilities of ontological nature of the focus of *Nirvāna*.

(1) *First Possibility Discussed*

When *Pūrvapakṣin* says that *Nirvāna* is ontologically existing Nāgārjuna repudiates his contention for following reasons :

(a) If *Nirvāṇa* is taken to be ontically existent, it would be then subject to decay and dissolution as whatever is ontically existent is so, for, decay and dissolution are invariable characters of ontic existence.[60]

(b) If *Nirvāṇa* is taken to be ontically existent complex[61] then we will be able to spell out its component factors. But we are unable to do so.

(c) If *Nirvāṇa* is taken to be ontically existent then it would be determined by sets of causes and conditions.[62] But since *Nirvāṇā* is uncompound (asaṃskṛta), not subject to decay, dissolution and being beyond all dependence, it follows that it is not and cannot be taken to be ontically existent.

(2) *Second possibility discussed :*

Pūrvapakṣin of Nāgārjuna, then argues that since *Nirvāṇa* is not ontically existent, does it not entail that it is ontically non-existent? Nāgārjuna immediately replies that ontic non-existence cannot be derived from denial of ontic existence. For, if it were ontically non-existent then how could it be legitimately said as beyond all dependence?[63] In that case, it will have to (logically) depend upon 'ontically existent' for its meaningfulness, like the dependence of predicate on subject. Hence the possibility under consideration cannot be acceptable as a description of *Nirvāṇa*.

(3) *Third possibility discussed :*

Pūrvapakṣin of Nāgārjuna says that granted, for the sake of argument, that first two possibilities cannot be accepted, but what difficulties would it embrace in conceding that *Nirvāṇa* is ontically existent and ontically non-existent as well? Nāgārjuna remarks that this view cannot be upheld on the following grounds :

(i) To say that *Nirvāṇa* is ontically existent and ontically non-existent is a contradiction.

(ii) To hold such a view means to admit cojointly the consequences of earlier two positions which, when considered separately, have been rejected as philosophically unwarrantable.

(iii) To accept *Nirvāṇa* as ontically existent as well as ontically non-existent leads to accept that final release would be both existent and non-existent.[64]

To explain the point under consideration at a greater length, Nāgārjuna says that *Nirvāṇa* is ontically existent would mean that it is dependent on complex of causes and conditions and to say that it is ontically non-existent would mean that it is logically dependent upon ontic existence for its meaning.[65] But in that case, it will be nothing else but compound.[66] Since *Nirvāṇa* is uncompound this possibility cannot be acceptable.[67]

(4) *Fourth possibility discussed* :

At last, *Pūrvapakṣin*, when he sees that his each point is turned down, asks whether it would be acceptable that *Nirvāṇa* is neither ontically existent nor ontically non-existent ? Here, too, Nāgārjuna rejects the contention under consideration on logical grounds. For, he says, that if there were something that is ontically existent, it would be then sensible to say that there is something else that is ontically non-existent, Similarly, if there were something that is ontically non-existent, then by negating it one would get something as not non-existent. But there is no *Nirvāṇa* which is ontically existent and/or ontically non-existent. So the question of getting their negation simply does not arise. Hence, to say that *Nirvāṇa* is neither ontically existent nor ontically non-existent is not logically intelligible and therefore acceptable.[68]

Thus, taking a critical view of all the four possibilities about ontological status of *Nirvāṇa*, Nāgārjuna rejects[69] all of them and declares them to be a product of wrong conceptualization and mental fabrication. This being the case he ultimately warns that those who subscribe to such an existence, cycle of birth and death, immortality of soul and such other things will not come to obtain calm and peace.[70] They—ordinary people—are immature and having meagre intellectual power, are caught in the grip of illusory notions and consider putative existence to be real.[71]

The Nature of Nirvāṇa

From the above discussion it follows that various attempts have been made by *Pūravapakṣiu* to trap the focus of *Nirvāṇa* in the *laukika* structure. But in the ultimate analysis it is shown that the views marshalled by him are mistakes and embrase unsound philosophical position, In this connection Nāgārjuna extensively spells out 'what *Nirvāṇa* should not be mistaken with'. But his 'don't dos' treatment alone does not succeed in conveying the positive import of *Nirvāṇa*, and it become necessary to throw light on the affirmative side of *Nirvāṇa* so as to enable anybody to grasp the import of it systematically and cogently.

As it is already pointed out *Saṁvṛti* being centrally situated in the common mode of speech, act and understanding takes many things for granted. One such basic presupposition of *lokasaṁvṛtti* is the cycle of birth and death and our taking of arising and passing away of things[72] as real phenomena. People carry out their day-to-day transaction under the impression that coming and going of the things is based on the complex of causes and conditions.[73] To evade the effect of such a *Loka vyavahāra*, which is deep rooted in the common parlance and deprives them to see and comprehend the nature of the world as it is, Nāgārjuna argues it is necessary to adopt a proper focus of *Nirvāṇa*. *Nirvāṇa* as a focus of understanding the nature of the world and the things in it, consists in (i) *Apratīti* of *Ājavnjavibhāva* (coming and going of things) (ii) *Anupādāna of Ājavanjavibhāva* and (iii) *Apravṛtti* of *Ājavanjavibhāva*.[74] That is, one comes to develop a proper perspective provided one succeeds (a) in coming out of the impression that coming and going of the things is based on the set of causes ond conditions. ⟨b) in coming out of the impression that arising and passing away of the things is not based on the things themselves and (c) in knowing that the process of coming and going of the things and the cycle of birth and death as is considered traditionally is anything but not a causal process. Thus, the development of the focus of *Nirvāṇa* reveals to one the gap between fact and experience, experience and expectations, experience and knowledge and as a result one realizes the falsity of everyday transaction. Such a focus, then, becomes instrumental to (1) knowing the unreality of unreal objects and (2) the inappropriateness of the (present) language to describe the nature of discrete particular things. This further takes one to realize that the setback that one gets on the level of *Lokavyavahāra* is due to the a) Lack of making distinction between knowlege and experience[75] (b) the use of defective language, (c) the habit of illicit conceptualization and hypostatization ; (d) the employment of notions, ideas concepts without envisaging the real import of them. Thus, proper understanding of *Nirvāṇa* as a focus to 'view' or 'see' the things in the world leads to repose the entire manifold of the things—named and naming, the normal habit of concept formation[76] and there remains nothing for language to refer to. Thus, in Nirvāṇa as a focus, there is a distillation of all names, concepts, ideas and such things.[77] This is Nirvāṇa—a proper perspective—focus—utter dissipation of reifying thought[78]—the silence. In such a state of being does one destroy or suppress anything ? Not at all.[79] The question of destruction or suppression, after having adopted a focus of Nirvāṇa simply does not arise.[80] It is coming to rest all pervasive marks of everyday experience of a layman.[81]

Characteristics of Nirvāṇa :

Nirvāṇa—as a philosophical focus has to play an important role in the entire scheme of Buddha's philosophy and thereby philosophy of Nāgārjuna. It enables one to develop such an insight that it removes the proliferative ontology and misleading epistemological weed and reveals the nature of the reality as it is. Such a philosophically indespensable perspective, like *Pratītya Samutpāda*, Nāgārjuna characterizes[82] as follows :

1. *Aprahīnam* : *Nirvāṇa* as a philosophical focus is such that (though very difficult to adopt) once anopted it cannot be exterminated. Chandrakīrti tell us that Nirvāṇa is not like desires or affiictions[83] that arise and cease to exist in course of time. Once we develop a proper perspective, it never ceases to be for any reason. 2. *Asamprāptam* : Nirvāṇa as a focus is very difficult to capture as it requires a discipline of thinking. So far as the majority of the people is concerned as they fail to adopt it, it is away (asamprāpta) from them. When it is away from them, they are put in a philosophical loss as they are normally prone to commit errors and confusion. 3. *Anucchinnam* : As it is pointed out about *Pratītya Samutpāda*, it also holds good about Nirvāṇa. Nirvāṇa as a philosophical perspective, is to be understood differently from its traditional meaning as summum bonum or the highest bliss or ideal etc. When we develop such a proper perspective, we come to give up the traditional meaning of it. But that does not mean that all misunderstanding about it comes to an end. Those who fails to develop *Nirvāṇa* as such a perspective remain under the sway of its wrong interpretation and therefore it is called *anucchinna.*

4. *Aśāśvatam* : It should be understood differently. That it is

a focus and it needs to be adopted by a person. A person, who develops such a perspective, alone knows what is the nature of the world and things in it. He is also aware about the many things which otherwise are considered to be meaningful in our life. So, so far as particular person is concerned, after his death, the focus becomes null and void. It means that the development of such a perspective is not a transferable quality. This being the case, *Nirvāṇa* becomes a contingent feature. 5. *Anirodham* : *Nirvāṇa* is not a subject of cessation. It is a proper perspective 'to look at' the things in the world and once it is adopted it cannot be given up by lebelling that it is 'not required for practical purpose'. *Nirvāṇa* by its very nature is *aniruddha* and that such a perspective is so philasophically illuminating that it takes place without any distrubance. 6. *Anutpaannam* : As one does not make the world and things in it emerge, so, too, one does not make the perspective about it emerge. So to speak about its emergence is pointless. As a proper perspective, one neither generates nor invents it. One can only discover that such and such a focus can be adopted. That there is such a focus and one can adopt it is a permanent possibility open before us. That one does not adopt it is an error on the part of an individual in case of which one is bound to lose oneself in the fog of misunderstanding and miscomprehension of the nature of the world. Therefore, it is proper and desirable to think of its advent in order to save oneself falling into further confusion and (philosophical) errors.

Nirvāṇa ; Its Beariag upon Ontology

Every ontology is supposed to be comprehanded within an appropriate epistemology and is supposed to be captured within corresponding methodological framework. The latter two are explanatory devices with the help of which we seek to explain things, entities and individuals that are around us. The explanations of anything in this way we hope to be convergent. But our hope may come to be belled and as a result we may come to set up an epistemological and methodological framework that may deviate from the ontological boundary and the framework may, thus, turn out to be narrower or wider. In our epistemological enterprise we might fail to comprehend the boundary between experience and knowledge, we might also come to hold that everything methodologicatly worth the name must have an ontological anchorage. Ontology, epistemology and methodology are related with one another, but this in itself does not confer ontological status on everything that is epistemologically or logically significent. For instance, when one says that 'something is real' one need not presuppose that it is ontologically real i.e. existent. 'Some thing is real' itself can be employed on ontological, epistemological or logical level. That which is ontologically real has to be epistemologically or logically so but not conversely. The only [important point one must bear in mind is that an explanation of anything on these planes is a systematic effort made towards the acquisiton of knowledge and for that matter when such an explanation is put forth, one must see that it will not lead one to embarrasing a position that crosses the appropriate limits of its points of reference. This being the case, one will notice that various problems about the interpretation of *Nirvāṇa* have arisen out of the lack of understanding the proper frame of its explanation. That is, as a torch-bearer, it has indeed bearings upon ontological epistemological social field, but just on that ground it itself cannot be considered as ontological, epistemological, moral, social etc. Therefore, when Buddha's and Nāgārjuna's utterances like 'there is *Nirvāṇa* are largely interpreted by people as having ontological epistemological or social import, it is according to me, a mistaken view.

We have already elaborately dealt with the view that *Nirvāṇa* as a focus is not itself ontological. However, it does not mean that *Nirvāṇa* has no bearings on world or our knowledge of it, though on this ground *Nirvāṇa* itself does not fall within the range of ontological boundary of the world. Nor does it become an item in our knowledge of it. It, as a focus, has an immense methodological and regulative role to perform. It would, nonetheless, be interesting to study bearings of *Nirvāṇa* as a proper perspective on ontology and epistemology through its connection with *Pratītya Samutpāda* and *Śūnyatā*.

Nirvāṇa as a proper perspective, regulative of our habit, 'to view' things in the world has profound implications. When it is brought to bear upon the ontological sphere, one comes to know that all things which are commonsensically taken to be real are not so. Rather some items are real while many others are unreal. Those items which are ontologically there, i.e. which are said to inhabit the world are given to us in a rightly understood *Pratītya-*

samutpāda way. On the background of the genuine presentation of things in the way in which they happen to be taken to be given reveals the reality of only genuinely real items. But equally importantly it reveals the unreality of unreal items as well. Thus, on the ontological level, Nirvāṇa as a focus primarily seeks to do away those items which we deem to be there on commonsensical level and helps one to comprehend those and only those items which genuinely inhabit this world not simply because they alone constitute the world but their being there is also philosophically warrantable. No matter whichever perspective one adopts 'to see' them, they will stand there to be real. Thus, Nirvāṇa as a perspective does not make real things real; it rather brings to our notice the direction in which unreality of unreal things could be brought to surface.

Nirvāṇa : its Bearings Upon Epistemology

On epistemological level, when one 'looks at' through the focus of *Nirvāṇa*, one comes to realize unreality of illusory and hallucinatory objects. Further, it guides us to realize that the things in the world are no doubt given to us one after the other, but it forms merely 'sequence' among them and thus it leads to comprehension of unreality of the impression of 'consequence', which otherwise is taken to be the basic feature of the world. It is in this way that Nirvāṇa is said to be connected with *Pratītyasamutpāda* and both of them together are instrumental in enabling us to comprehend the nature of the world.

Nirvāṇa : its Bearings Upon Linguistic Frame

On linguistic level, the use of the focus of *Nirvāṇa* helps one to realise that the basic function of the language is itself defeated at its own ground, that, it is brought in practice for successful communication, but what it communicates is anything but the real nature of the world. Things in the world being uniquely particular and distinct from each other possess only *Svabhāvabhūta dharmas*. But due to the fact that language reveals only the shareable features, it fails to describe the real *dharmas* of things. The qualities which we happen to comprehend as possessed by things, through the employment of language, are *niḥsvabhāvabūta dharmas*. They are not there in the things. Thus, adoption of a proper perspective helps one to realize (i) futility of ordinary language and

(ii) unreality of *niḥsvabhāvabhūta dharmas*.[84] *Nirvāṇa* also points out the unreality of relation between words and the things in the world; i.e. it falsifies the impression that there are as many objects in the world as many words there are in the language. Thus, the adoption of the focus of *Nirvāṇa* helps one to cognize the unreality of unreal items and through the employment of the tool of *Śūnyatā* one comes to give up the proliferative part of ontology, epistemology and the use of defective language. It is in this way that *Nirvāṇa* is said to be connected with *Śūnyatā* and that one who adopts such a proper perspective—*Nirvāṇa*—is bound to wield a methodological tool—*Śūnyatā* to cut off the ontological, epistemological and linguistic slum to cleanse the way towards the comprehension of reality, which itself converges upon that world-view which is given to us through the rightly understood *Pratītyasamutpāda* way. Thus, if the world is said to be comprised of real and unreal items and if unreal items are done away with through the operation of Śūnyatā what remains behind are those and only those items that are genuinely real and their nature, structure and constitution would be brought to our notice by rightly understood *Pratītyasamutpāda*. It is in this way if the former is shown to be related with *Nirvāṇa* the latter can also be shown to be related with it.

Nirvāṇa : its Bearings Upon Social Moral and Religious Fields :

On this line of thinking, when one applies this perspective to the social and religious fields, one comes to analyse the common mode of behaviour, the nature of social, moral and religious problems and the interconnection between them in a better way. The adoption of proper perspective reveals the unreality of these problems and thereby an individual comes to give up unduly being concerned about these problems. Likewise, one does not take them to be part of the ontological world. It does not mean that a person who develops such a perspective shows negligence towards social, moral and religious problems. In fact a person having developed such a focus gives due respect to these problems. After all, he is to live in the same society. So far as the social pattern of behaviour is concerned, such a person will have to accept social framework for his day-to-day life. But when these problems are considered from ontological point of view, particularly through their bearings upon the nature and structure of the world, such considerations drive him to admit that these problems do not have any power 'to influence' or 'to change' the structure and the constitution of the world and as such, have no ontological anchorage. Since all of them are *niḥsvabhāvabhūta*,[85] they can be modified if they infringe upon man-nature or man-man relationship. It happens so because there is difference between a commonsensical approach and an approach of such a person endowed with such a perspective. There is a vast difference in their insight and understanding. That is why anybody looking at the world through this perspective need not take everything that is commonsensically significant to be philosophically so. Similarly, whatever one takes as socially, morally or religiously significant in common parlance need not be taken to be so ontologically and philosophically. For, they are all anthropocentric devices of ordering behaviour and modes of fellowship of individuals and are not immutable. This being the case, although it makes sense to say that we shall never be in a position to get rid of genuinely real things, yet it does not make sense to say that social, moral or religious considerations cannot be altered and that they have to be adhered to as once they have been formulated and laid down. That is why a person having developed a proper perspective may not necessarily respect every thing philosophically—everything that is accepted by commonsense understanding. Though the process of commonsense explanation and philosophic explanation aim at acquisition of knowledge yet the knowledge of a common man is not always a certified true belief, nor is it amenable to the kind of cognitive systematization it should be. This is due to the lack of systematic study and profoundity in layman's insight. So it results into the failure of pointing out the unreality of unreal items and thus leads to the acceptance of everything that is social, moral, religious to be as real as a genuine ontological item. But when a person develops the focus of *Nirvāṇa* he automatically relizes the changeability of social, moral and religious problems and considerations and hence has no hesitation to embark upon *Dharmacakrapravatana* as the Buddha did. It does not then require any drill and parade for one's coming to develop such a perspective, although once one comes to develop it, it brings in implications of very profound significance.

Thus, those items which one deems to be real on ontological, epistemological or social planes are taken into account as part and parcel of the furniture of the world on the level of *Saṁvṛtti*, need to be segregated from those items which are genuinely real. For, such a kind of treatment is not only helpful to avoid the consideration that the world, which one normally is accustomed to, is a kind of hold-all, but is also essential to comprehend the real nature of the world. One who comprehends the nature of *Nirvāṇa* as a philosophical perspective in this way, dares not form his view about the nature of the world in a commonsensical way. For, he very well knows that such a kind of description of the world is partial and never succeeds in describing the world as it is. Thus, *Nirvāṇa* as a focus or a philosophical perspective functions as an instrument to perspectival nullification,[86] leading towards the philosophical path—*Madhyamā Pratipad*—a real mean between two extreme position like *sarvāstivāda* and *Śūnyavāda* (in the traditional sense of the term), stability and change, materialism v/s ascetism, excessive enjoyment v/s self-mortification etc., which are denied as the theories of reality by the Buddha and also by Nāgārjuna. It is the *Nirvāṇa*—the focus or the perspective alone which enables one to adopt the middle way as a philosophical position by giving up each and very misleading and extreme view[87] regarding the nature of reality. It now remains to see, what constitutes the middle way and what are the repurcussions of it on various levels of understanding but that we will see in the next chapter.

NOTE

1. See Chapter 2.

2. Sprung, M., (ed.); *"The problem of two truths in Buddhism & Vedanta"*, p. 46.

3. *Madhyamakaśāstra*, 27.29.

4. *Prasannapadā;* on 24,18 Yah ca svabhvāena anutpādaḥ bhavānām sā Śūnyatā.

5. *Madhyamakaśāstra;* 13.8 and Prasannapada on it.
    Śūnyatā sarva dṛṣṭinām proktā nihsaranam jinaih/
    Yeṣām tu śūnyatā dṛṣṭih tān asādhyān babhāsire//

6. *Prasannapadā* on 15.11: Na vidyate sattā svabhāvah sarvabhā-

vānāmityabhāvāḥ sarvadharmāḥ sunyāḥ sarvadharmā niḥs-vabhavayogena iti.

7. *Madhyamakaśāstra* 24.18 and Prasannapadā on it.

8. *Prasannapadā*; Introduction to the 27th chapter. "Pratītya samutpādasya yathāvadavasthitatatvadarsanāt nānyathāvasthitaṁ vastu anyathā abhiniviśate/"

9. *Prasannapadā* on 18.5 also *Catuḥsatakaṁ* 12.23.

10. *Prasannapadā* on 24.7 "... Pratītya samutpādasya yaḥ arthaḥ sa eva śūnyatā śabdasya arthaḥ Also *Madhyamakaśāstra* 24.18.

11. Kalupahana D., *Buddhist Philosophy—A Historical Analysis*, p. 69.

12. Ketkar G.V., '*Maharashtriya Jñānakośa*', Vol. IV, p. 189.

13. *Saṁyukta Nikāya*; (Nalanda-Devanagari Pali Text Series hereinafter NDPS) "...Rogakkhayo Dosakkhya Mohakkhayo its vuñcati Nibbāna/" Vol. IV, p. 223.

14. *Dīgha Nikāya*; (NDPS) "... Tanhākkh virāgo nirodho Nibbanaṁ/" Vol II, p. 30. Cf *Anguttara Nikāya;* (NDPS), Vol. IV, pp. 61-62.

15. Ketkar, G.V., '*Maharashtriya Jñānakośa*', Part IV 'Buddhot-tara Jaga', p. 127.
'त्यामुले सर्व दुःखांचा शेवट होउन अत्युच्य सुख जे निर्वाण त्याचा अनुभव मिलतो.''

16. *Milinda Panho* (in Devanagari) (ed. R.D. Wadekar), Bombay, 1940, pp.

17. Pande, G.C., "*Studies in Origins of Buddhism*", p. 445.

18. Ketkar, G.V., '*Maharashtriya Jñānakośa*', Part IV, 'Buddhot-tara Jaga', p. 190.

19. Sprung, M. (ed.) '*The Problem of two truths in Buddhism and Vedānta*', p. 33.

20. Monier, W., "*Buddhism*", p. 544.

21. Poussin, La De. V. Nirvāna (ERE) Vol. IX, pp. 376-78.

22. Monier, W., *Buddhism*, 544.

23. Sprung, M., *'Lucid Exposition of the Middle Way'*, p. 19.

24. *Madhyamakaśāstra*, 25.1
   Yadi śūnyamidaṁ sarvamudayo nāsti na vyayaḥ/
   Prahāṇādvā nirodhādvā kasya nirvāṇamiṣyate//

25. Poussin La De V., Nirvāṇa (Buddhist) ERE Vol. IX, p. 377.

26. Keith, A.B., *Buddhist Philosophy*, p. 67.

27. Dahlke, Paul; *Buddhist Essays* (Tr. by Bhikku Śīlācāra from German) pp. 85-86.

28. Dasgupta, S.N., *History of Indian Philosophy*, Vol. I, p. 75.

29. Radhakrishnan, S., *Indian Philosophy*, Vol. I, p. 603.

30. Stcherbatsky, Th., *The Concept of Buddhist Nirvāṇa.* pp. 63, 68.
   also Joshi, G.N., *Atman and Mokṣa*, p. 159
   also Hiriyanna, M., *Outline of Indian Phiiosophy*, p. 152.

31. Monier, W., *Buddhism*, p. 139

32. There are many such examplcs of utter non-existence in the commentary of Candrakīrti. To augment the list one can add "donkey's horns; odor of sky-flower; mirage; horns of hares, etc."

33. *Prasannapadā*; "...... saṁsārasatbhāve tu sati iha krtasya karmaṇo janmāntaraḥ api vipāka phala sambandhāt karmaṇām ... ", p. 132.

34. *Ibid,* " ... abhipdāna abhidheya jñānajñeyādi vyavahārah aśeṣaḥ Lokasaṁvṛttisatyaṁ iti ucchyate/", p. 215.

35. *Prasannapadā.* Vidyate eva skandhāyatanadhātavaḥ/ p. 55.
   Vidyate eva saṁskṛtasvabhāvāḥ/ p. 59.
   Vidyate eva ātmā/ p. 100.
   Vidyate eva bhāvānām svabhavaḥ/ p. 123.
   Vidyate eva saṁsāraḥ/ p. 132.

36. *Ibid,* Ajñānaṁ hi samantāt ... saṁvṛttirityuccyate paraspara sambhavanaṁvā saṁvṛttiḥ/ p. 215.

37. *Ibid,* Na hi paramārthataḥ ete vyavahārāḥ saṁbhavantti, p. 215.

38. *Ibid*, Sa hi parmārthaḥ aparpratyayaḥ śāntaḥ *pratyātmavedya*
    āryāṇām sarvaprapañeātītaḥ/ p. 215.

39. *Ibid*, Sa nopadiśyate na cāpi jñāyate/ p. 215.

40. Refrainment from the use of ordinary language is due to its
    very defective structure. It does not mean thnt there is noth-
    ing to describe. In fact Nāgārjuna admits that there are
    discrete particular things and can be legitimately considered
    in principle, to be the objects of description. But his difficulty
    is that the language which we normally use is imperfect and
    imprecise. Therefore, there is no alternative than to abstain
    from description of such a world in ordinary language. Were
    we to fashion a language, Nāgārjuna would argue, suitable
    for our being able to describe uniquely particular things then
    perhaps we would be able to describe the things in the world.
    But in so far as there is no such a suitable language at our
    disposal and when we are armed with the defective linguistic
    tool, must we not be pretty cautious about its careful use ?
    Otherwise, wielding it in a wrong manner may perhaps
    boomrang upon us and (philosophically) ruin us *Madhyama-
    kaśāstra*, 24.11). Thus, refrainment from the use of the kind
    of language which we are normally prone to use is indicative
    of not silence but only cautiousness. It means that argu-
    ments fashioned and articulated in ordinary language do not
    have validity for *Paramārthasatya*. Nāgārjuna is not a scep-
    tic or a nihilist. He is not denying there is any real thing
    at all. *Mādhyamikas* could never accept strict prohibition to
    talk about *Paramārthasatya*. They rather intend to draw our
    attention to the fact that ordinary language that we have is
    ill-suited for the purpose.

41. *Madhyamakaśāstra* 25.20.

    "Nirvāṇasya ca yā kotiḥ kotiḥ samsaraṇasya ca
    na tayorantarm kiñcit susūkṣmamapi vidyate//"

42. *Ibid*, 25.19.

    Na Samsārasya nirvāṇat kiñcit asti viśeṣaṇam/
    na Nirvāṇasya samsārāt kiñcit asti viśeṣaṇam//

43. Sprung, M., *"Lucid Exposition of the Middle Way"*, p. 260.

44. *Prasannapadā*" ...Saṁsāranirvaṇayoḥ janyajanako bhāvo dṛṣṭah iti"/p. 172.

45. Sprung, M. (Ed.); "*The Problem of Two Truths in Buddhism and Vedanta*", p. 19.

46. *Prasannapadā;*" ... Paramārthaḥ niṣprapañca svabhāvaḥ"/ p. 215.

47. *Ibid*, "Tat etat satyadvayaṁ āśritya Buddhānāṁ dharmadeśana pravartate/" p. 215.

48. *Madhyamakaśāstra* 18.
Nāgārjuna critically considers the view of Pūrvapakṣin that there is Ātmā—a substratum of various activities and ultimately rejects it.

49. *Prasannapadā*; pp. 128-29.

50. *Madhyamakaśāstra*, 16.4 and *Prasannapadā* on it.

51. *Prasannapadā*; '...Yat api idaṁ anutpannān sarvadharmān... ca utpādayati/', p. 130.

52. *Ibid*, "... svapnopalabdha dahanajvālā nirvāpaṇavat tat anilasalilaiḥ iti/" p. 131.

53. *Ibid*, "Saṁsāranirvāṇayoḥ anupalabhyamānatvāt/", p. 130.

54. *Ibid*, "Vidyate eva saṁsāraḥ, ... tasmāt asti saṁsāraḥ/" p. 125.

55. Candrakirti uses such expressions as 'gaganakusumasaurabha' or 'khapuṣpasaugandha' to show their inconceivability, that there is no difficulty in aceepting it as inconceivable.

56. *Prasannapadā;* Na hi anupalabhya vandhyāduhitaraṁ ... rāgiṇaḥ/ p. 150.

57. *Ibid*, Tadevaṁ nirvāṇaṁ api nāsti tat abhāvāt na asti saṁsāraḥ/ p. 126.

58. *Ibid*, Ye tu ... bhāvābhāvatadubhayānubhayarupaṁ nirvānaṁ parikalpayanti tān prati uccyate/ p. 229.

59. *Ibid*, ... Jaiminikāṇādakāpiladināṁ vaibhaṣika paryantāṁ .../ p. 229.

60. *Ibid*, bhāvasya jarāmaraṇalakṣaṇa avyabhicāritvāt/ p. 230.

61. *Madhyamakaśāstra;* 25.5 and Prasannapadā on it.
    Yadi nirvāṇaṁ bhāvaḥ syāt, tadā tat nirvāṇaṁ saṁskṛtaṁ bhavet/ p. 230.

62. *Prasannapadā;* Svakāraṇasāmagrimāśritya bhavet ityarthaḥ/ p. 230.

63. I*bid*, 'Yadi bhavasca nirvāṇaṁ ... /' p. 231.

64. *Ibid*, 'Yadi bhāvābhāvobhayarupaṁ nirvāṇaṁ syāt ... / p. 232.

65. *Ibid*, " ... upādāyaiva bhavati na anupādāya", p. 232.

66. *Ibid*, "Tat yadi bhāvābhāuasvabhāvaṁ nirvāṇaṁ syāt, tadā naa saṁskṛtaṁ; (Kiṁ tu) Saṁskṛtaṁ eva/", p. 233.

67. *Ibid*, "Bhāvābhāvayoḥ api parasparaviruddhayoḥ ekstra nirvāṇe nāsti sambhava iti, ataḥ" bhavet bhavo ... kathaṁ/" naiva bhavet iti abhiprāyaḥ/" p. 233.

68. *Prasannapadā*; "Tasmāt na Kenacinnirvāṇe naivābhāvo naiva bhāva ityajyate/", p. 234.

69. *Ibid*, "Sarvathā yathā ca nirvāṇe etāścatasraḥ kalpanā na saṁbhavati/", p. 234.

70. *Samādhiraja Sūtra*; 9. 26.
    Astīti nāstīti ca kalpanāvatāṁ
    Evaṁ Carantāṁ na duḥkha śāmyati/

71. Sprung, M., *"Lucid Exposition of the Middle Way"*, p. 250.

72. *Prasannapadā*; "Tatra ājavanjavībhāvaḥ agamangamanabhāvajanmamaraṇaparaṁparetyarthaḥ/" p. 231.

73. *Ibid*, ... kadācit hetupratyayasāmagrīṁ āśritya astīti prajñapyate ityarthaḥ/" p. 231.

74. *Madhyamakaśāstra*, 25.9 and Prasannapadā on it.
    Ya ājavanjavībhāva upādāya pratītya vā/
    So 'pratītyānupādāya nirvaṇamupadiśyate//

75. Carnap, R., *"Library of Living Philosophers"*, (Ed.) by Schilpp, P.A., Vol. XI, p. 38.

76. *Prasannapadā*, " ... prapañcānāṁ nimittānāṁ ya upaśamo' pravṛttistannirvāṇaṁ/" p. 236.

77. *Ibid*, "Tataśca niravaśeṣa kalpanākṣaya rupaṁ eva nirvāṇaṁ/"
    p. 228.

78. *Ibid*, 'Tataśca Sarvakalpanākśayarupaṁ eva nirvāūam'/ p.
    229.

79. *Ibid*, "Tadevaṁ nirvāṇe na kasyacit prahānaṁ nāpi kasyacin-
    nirodhaḥ iti vijñeyaṁ"/ p. 228.

80. *Ibid*, Tat svabhāvato' niruddhamanutpannaṁ ca ... /" p. 228.

81. *Ibid*, "Nirvāṇaṁ iti bhagavan yaḥ praśamaḥ sarvanimittānāṁ
    uparatiḥ/", p. 237.

82. *Madhyamakaśāstra*; 25.3.

83. *Prasannapadā*; "Yat hi naiva prahīyate rāgādivat"/ p. 228.

84. *Prasannapadā*; Śūnyāḥ sarvadharmā niḥsvabhāvayogena/
    p. 218.

85. Prasannapadā, Karmakartṛphalādikaṁ ... niḥsvabhāvameta-
    diti vyavasthāpayāmaḥ/
    p. 142.

86. *Madhyamakaśāstra* 13.8.
    Śūnyatā sarvadṛṣṭināṁ proktā niḥsaraṇaṁ jinaiḥ/
    Yeṣāṁ tu śūnyatā dṛṣṭistānasādhyān babhāṣire//

87. *Ibid*, 27.30.
    Sarvadṛṣṭiprahāṇāya yaḥ saddharmamadeśayat
    Anukaṁpāmupādāya taṁ namasyāmi gautamaṁ.//

CHAPTER V

MADHYAMĀ PRATIPAD

Śūnyavāda is not Nāgārjuna's Philosophical Position

In the preceeding chapter we considered the problem of *Nirvana* as Nāgārjuna expects us to understand. The argument we put forward, there, is : *Nirvāṇa* is understood both by the Buddha and Nāgārjuna as a proper perspective or a philosophical focus that everybody needs to develop for the proper understanding of the nature of the world and things in it. *Nirvāṇa*, as a proper perspective, enables one to see the things in the world, develop an entirely different outlook about the world and in that sense differs considerably from its traditional meaning that it is an ethical or religious ideal to be cherished or accomplished by man. The so-called religiocity which we bring in the focus of *Nirvāṇa* is due to our misunderstanding and confusion. This is not to deny that there are important problems in human life regarding which social, moral or even religious considerations do not arise. But it is important to understand that in considering *Nirvāṇa* to be essentially a religious or moral phenomenon we come to highlight such aspect of it that appears to be peripheral, especially in its philosophical significance, and thereby cloud the entire philosophic atmosphere. It is this latter that must be set aside as judiciously as possible. This is again not to say that *Nirvāṇa* as a philosophical perspective has nothing whatever to do with social, moral or even religious aspects of human life. But to say that such a perspective arises basically, if not exclusively, out of the latter kind of consideration is to claim, in our view, little too much. For, as pointed out in the preceeding chapter, given that *Nirvāṇa* is connected with *Pratītya-samutpāda* and *Śūnyatā*, understanding the former as religious or moral ideal forces us to understand the latter two also in the same spirit. It is this, which, in our opinion, is distortive. Instead, we endeavoured to understand each of them philosophically and study interrelationship between them. We argued that a person, who rightly understands *Nirvāṇa* not as an ideal nor even as an end of life but as a philosophical focus in the light of which we are supposed to understand the nature of the world basically as it is rather than as it appears to be, cognizes the futility of explanation of Nirvāṇa basically in terms of social, moral or religious frameworks and brands them to be merely anthropocentric device employed for whatever reason they might have been brought in. A person, having understood thus that the real nature of the world cannot appropriately be captured by the kind of language we have at our disposal, turns cautious about it and rightly refrains from embarking upon misleading, if not altogether wrong, description of the world. Now it would indeed be good if people were dissociated from such acts of wrong description and free from falling into further confusion and error. But, however, mere pious expectations of this kind do not in themselves guarantee emergence of the corresponding situation as a matter of fact. As a result, people continue to be engaged in describing the nature of the world and things in it as they please ! One such account is that the world has the features of change and continuity, perhaps as its structural features. Accordingly, there arises a problem of giving a satisfactory account of them. Philosophers right from ancient times have made persistent attempts to account for these features of the world and in consequence have come to put forth theories which are at variance from one another, if not dimetrically opposed. Philosophers of one camp emphasised change at the cost of continuity while those of other camp highlighted continuity to such an extent that change as the feature of the world come bluntly to be denied or else it is considered to be its merely apparent, if not functional, feature. Consequently, according to those, who consider change alone to be the structural feature of the world, continuity of the world is such a feature of it which can, at the most, be taken to be a quality of attribution than that of possession. In other worlds, they hold that continuity is something that we attribute to the world although it does not have continuity as a structural feature of it. On the other hand, some other philosophers have disallowed change to be the structural feature of the world and have held that it is not ceaseless change (alone) that is the structural feature of it. It is rather continuity which is the structural feature that belongs to it. In the intellectual climate of a given philosophic tradition some or the other of these views has received an upper hand and as a result one finds this kind of tendency being fairly represented in both the philosophical major traditions-oriental or accidental. Accordingly, even if one delimits to oriental philosophical tradition in general and Indian philosophical tradition in particular, one finds both these views to have been upheld in vying opposition and antagonism to each other. Sometimes else, however, one notices such philosophical trends wherein instead of emphasing change and neglecting continuity or conversely both change and continuity are together considered to be structural features of the world. For instance, at the hands of philosophers of the *Sānkhya* School[1] it is continuity that seems to be considered as a stable feature of the world while in *Śaṁkara Vedānta*,[2] both change and continuity are considered to be structural features of the world. Consider again *Nayāy*[3] and Buddhism. There, discreteness seems to be considered to be the hallmark of the world rather than its organic unity as the basic characteristic of it. In Buddhism in particular, again, right from the teaching of the Buddha it is change which is considered to be the basic feature of the world while continuity is taken to be the functional feature of it. Behind such panorama of views there is seen an urge to account for such a feature of the world that is structural and constitutive of it. But the fact remains that of all the features of the world that have attracted philosophers' prolonged attention, the features of change and continuity have remained foremost and in the various explanations that have been offered by philosophers, roughly, either change or continuity is taken to be the basic feature of the world.[4]

On this background, we showed that *Pratītyasamutpāda*, which is the principal teaching of the Buddha and which is also instrumental in freeing us from bewitching platonic world-view is commonsensically enormously misinterpreted at the hands of the scholars, no matter whether hailling from the Buddhist camp or not. They mistook *Pratītyasamutpāda* for a theory of causation or a theory of emergence of the things in the world or a theory of their dependent origination. Our claim is that as a true teaching of the Buddha it only points out the way things in the world truly are and stand related to one another. It is, thus, on ontological model explaining not necessarily emergence and perishing of things in the world but rather their presentation unto us conjunctively or

sequentially. It further tells us that the continuity which we feel
is perhaps the functional feature of the world. That we feel it and
congnize it is not a matter of discovery. Nor could continuity,
perhaps, be regarded as the structural feature of the world.
Continuity, perhaps, is our name for things being connected.
Things may, as a matter of fact, be discrete. They may be given to
us sequentially. They may even be related with one another; they
may not be related in this way. But merely from the fact that
things are related, it does not follow that continuity is the structural
feature of the world. We experience sequence and this sequence no
doubt gives us an idea of connectedness (No one should deny it
nor does the Buddha deny it.) But this connectedness should not be
mistaken for causal connectedness, which further implies that
sequence also should not be mistaken for consequence. This is the
true import of *Pratītyasamutpāda*. But unfortunately the disciples
of the Buddha and also scholars of his thought took *Pratītya
Samutpāda* for causal connectedness. This being the case, Nāgārjuna makes an honest attempt to understand *Pratītāsamutpāda*
correctly as a theory about the nature of the things in the world
and their being connected with one another.

As *Pratītyasamutpāda* comes to be misunderstood and distorted
so too the notion *Śūnyatā*—a methodological tool wielded
by Nāgārjuna to do away with the proliferative ontology,
and through such a kind of weeding out of items that do not
properly belong to the world to pave for the proper understanding
of it. But here, too, there is a lot of misunderstanding. That is
why dealing with it in the third chapter we showed that its traditional interpretation, in the strict literal sense, is not at all intended
by the Buddha. It is not intended by Nāgārjuna either. Nor
could he have intended it and in the same breath talked of properly
understanding the world and things in it. It is rather a consequence
of confusion and error. Scholars simply mistook *Śūnyatā* for
abhāva and branded Nāgārjuna ās *Śūnyavādin* (nihilist). Nāgārjuna
however, does not characterise his philosophical position as
Śūnyaavdā even once in the entire text of *Madhyamakaśātar*. Even
in other works of his, he has nowhere characterised his philosophical position in that way. Ratnakīrti, his commentator, though
come centuries after him, is equally emphatic in repudiating their
philosophical position being taken as *Śūnyavadā*. As was argued
earlier, it seems to us that *Śūnyatā* being a methodological weapon

is required to be wielded from a philosophical perspective in such a way that it should tailor the otherwise proliferative growth of ontology. It is also designed to bring home to us number of inadequacies our language suffers from and thereby convince us that the very conceptual framework that we often and normally employ to characterise and map the world adds confusion to errors whereby we remain farther removed from clarity, unambiguity and precision. Nāgārjuna we argued, through bringing in *Śūnyatā* wants to impress upon us that very often our language does not give us a true picture of the world and the world [often lacks those features which our language ascribes to it. To say this is not an invitation to give up language but to use it with utmost caution and care. Instead of saying that the world has the features which our language reveals, it would be philosophically more worthwhile to see our language can reveal unmistakenly those features that the world has. That is, the problem that is of paramount importance is how shall we come to describe the world as it is, without any commission or omission. *Śūnyatā* is thus, not meant to tell us that the world is empty. It is failure to understand this as also unmindfulness about Nāgārjuna's repeated protests against understanding his view to be nihilistic that led people to hold a view about *Śūnyatā* 'that is characteristically at variance from Nāgārjuna's understanding. Going this way Nāgārjuna was made to uphold a view that he does not wish to. This being the case, we outlined the reasons as to why Śūnyatā needs to be understood as a methodological tool and brought out its nature and significance when understood that way. We saw that through the methodological tool—*Śūnyatā*—Nāgārjuna tells us why we should understand the world the way he wants us to understand it and what is wrong with the way we normally are prone to understand. It, thus, does not give us an empty world that is inhabited by nothing but rather the world that is inhabited by those and only those things that as a matter of fact belong to it. We, thus, saw that in Nāgārjuna's philosophical framework *Pratītyasamutpāda Śūnyatā* and *Nirvāṇa* stand related in such way that none of them can be so separated from the rest of the two. If and in so far as we tend to do that we come to caricuture his philosophy rather than properly understand it. It is this kind of error and misunderstanding, we pointed out, into which considerable number of studies in Nāgārjuna's philosophy have, unfortunately, fallen. Be that as it may.

But it may be asked, why does Nāgārjuna bring in *Pratītya Samutpāda, Śūnyatā* and *Nirvāṇa* and what object does he want to accomplish through pointing out the sort of interconnection between them that he presents. Pointing out such an interconnection between them is important but cannot be said to be philosophically interesting unless it is shown to be bearing upon something that is philosophically illuminating and rewarding. It is this kind of bearing of them that would give them an added significance. We want to argue that the entire exercise is directed at our being able to develop a certain philosophical position and it is within the framework of such a philosophical position that the sort of interrelationship between *Pratītyasamutpāda, Śūyatā* and *Nirvāṇa* that we outlined in the previous chapters is said to gather its characteristic significance. It is further noteworthy that according to Nāgārjuna that philosophical position that he presents is not his own but rather the one that the Buddha wanted people to adopt. Thus, it is the position to which the Buddha himself subscribed. It is towards development of such a philosophical position that the three— *Pratītyasamutpāda, Śūnyatā*, and *Nirvāṇa* and interrelationship between them is said to be instrumental. That one should come to develop a proper philosophical position is the philosophically interesting goal, a road which requires an employment of a methodological tool, a proper philosophical focus and a philosophically worthwhile understanding of the world. If anyone of them is lacking so much the worse and the consequence would be that he would fail to understand the message of the Buddha. Hence Nāgārjuna endeavours to outline the sort of philosophical position the Buddha wanted us to adopt and it is to give a sketch of it that we turn in this chapter.

Nāgārjuna's Philosophical Position

Nāgārjuna calls his philosophical position as '*Madhyamā Pratipad*' and characteristically names his treatise as *Madhyamakaśāstra* meaning thereby a work in which the philosophy of *Madhyamā Pratīpad* is expounded. In spite of however, Nāgārjuna's characterization of his philosophical position to be *Madhyamā Pratipad* and even though he repeatedly tells us that, through negligence, (deliberate) distortions and misunderstanding not only appropriate characterization but also unerroneous framework of it remained hidden and in consequence it came to be improperly characterised as nihilism, absolutism, monism, mysticism and what not[5] at the hands of various scholars. In the face of such kind of misunderstanding it becomes necessary to inquire as to how does Nāgārjuna characterize his philosophical position and why does he do that the way he does and what is wrong with the traditional characterization of it. With this end in view we endeavour to put forth our own understanding of what *Madhyamā Pratipad* stands for, as we get to know it from the text of *Madhyamakaśāstra*. This kind of investigation is but necessary in order to get to know the philosophical framework within which Nāgārjuna is trying to solve or dissolve some philosophically important problems. We will attempt to show that *Madhyamā Pratipad* of Nāgārjuna is a hint[6] to those who try to capture and map the reality within the fold of convenient 'isms' with the help of present language, projections, schema and conceptual frameworks which distort and disfigure the landscape to be mapped and do violence to the contours which should matter most in an understanding of the world that is philosophically worthwhile.

Before we take up the principal task in hand it is necessary to clarify a point. It is sometimes held that behind the advocacy of *Madhyamā Pratipad* to be the true characterisation of the philosophic teaching of the Buddha, the aim of Nāgārjuna was to oust metaphysics from the field of philosophy. But what seems to us more appropriate is that Nāgārjuna wanted to restore the philosophy of the Buddha to its proper status. The way in which he undertakes the job, might have resulted into ouster of certain sort of metaphysics; but for that both Nāgārjuna as well as the Buddha were hardly to be blamed. Really speaking Nāgārjuna did not carry out any efforts to oust any metaphysics from the field of philosophy. He, rather, pointed out that certain metaphysical problems we are prone to entertain can hardly be said to be warrantable and defensible within the philosophical position that the Buddha exhorted us to adopt. Instead of trying to entertain and warrant them in a philosophically indefensible way or instead of being carried away by linguistic and conceptual traps, emphasizing this or that side of the issue and commit a fallacy of commission, it is better that we give them up. At the hands of Nāgārjuna, in this way, what resulted is not ouster of metaphysics proper but of metaphysics improper[7] and for undertaking this kind of exercise we should indeed be grateful to Nāgārjuna rather than blame him. But ignoring this either conveniently or due to lack proper understanding, scholars and critics of Buddhism went on abusing Nāgārjuna for doing the job, which he did not at all do. To cherish a wrong perspective about the nature and structure of reality is itself erroneous and to beat drum aloud for the non-destructions of such a perspective and blame the person who destroys it is doubly erroneous. What Nāgārjuna intended to show is that the reality which we often conceive is conceived by us erroneously and misleadingly. What we get in and through the employment of the kind of language we are accustomed to, is not reality but a delusion of it. So, Nāgārjuna designs a method of teaching the philosophy of the Buddha in such a way that at once resolves many metaphysical and epistemological issues that were inherited, perhaps, from the Brahmanic tradition and unfortunately strengthened at the hands of *Pre-mādhyamika* scholars after the death of the Buddha.

Two Iterpretatios of Buddha's Silence

Though Buddha's silence on certain issues was very significant and pronounced and was itself an indicative of inappropriateness of certain metaphysical issues, later on it became the fountain head of those very issues. When the Buddha was personally delivering the speeches, he was repudiating the Brahmanic tradition and misconceptions that it gave rise to. But at the same time he was maintaining silence over controversial metaphysical issues. In such a situation, though people were listening him attentively and quietly, it does not mean that they were not alert to Buddha's strategy of answering some questions while overlooking others. People also observed that the Buddha keeps silence particularly on certain kind of metaphysical problems. And it might be the case that either out of scholarship of Buddha or out of reverence towards him people did not bring up to him the issue of metaphysical problems that bothered them. But soon after passing away of the Buddha, the controversy about Buddha's teaching—particularly his silence on metaphysical issues—appears to have come up forcefully to the foreground and on the meaningful interpretation of Buddha's silence, disciples were divided into two prominent groups. One of them appears to have held a view that since such a scholarly and enlightened person—the Bnddha—keep silence on metaphysical issues—particularly the nature of the universe etc. from an ultimate point of view there must not be anything to be significantly talked about and hence real. Had be anything to say, he would have said it. But as he did not say anything it means that there is nothing significantly and meaningfully to be spoken of. Thus, his silence is truthfully indicative of utter nihilism. Thus, 'Sarvaṁ Śūnyaṁ' is not perhaps the utterances that directly come from the horse's mouth but was perhaps the corollary of Buddha's silence. In this way Buddha's silence over metaphysical issues particularly seems to have laid *Pūrvapakṣin* of Nāgārjuna to hold that according to the Buddha there is nothing or nothing is real *i.e.*, nothing exists. This is the classic interpretation not only of 'Sarvaṁ Śūnyaṁ' but is also held to be the official position of the Buddha.

On the other hand, those, who did not subscribe to the view that Buddha's silence is an indication of his nihilistic approach to the reality, thought that the Buddha had nothing to repudiate and reject. Had he anything to reject he should have made it clear. But as he did not clearly say that something is unreal or non-existent it means that everything is real. It further meant that not only those items which are genuinely real are there but also those which we deem to be there are there, no matter whether they really have any ontological status or not. This kind of thinking, on the silence of the Buddha led people to consider the objects of normal perception, illusion and hallucination on par with each other, equally existent and having the same status and reality. Thus, Buddha's silence on metaphysical issue is significant, according to this view, for it indicates that the Buddha had nothing to reject. Thus, 'Sarvaṁ asti'—everything exists—become a truthful interpretation of Buddha's silence, which led people to consider the world as a hold-all of all kinds of things, which are real according to Buddha.

These two positions on Buddha's silence were far from Buddha's teaching. They were then known, perhaps as *Śūnyavāda* and *Sarvāstivāda* respectively. It is this situation which compelled Nāgārjuna to repudiate both *Śūnyavāda* and *Sarvāstivāda*—the so-called official positions of Buddha's philosophy which emerged out of the convenient interpretation of Buddha's silence at the hands of his disciples. For, both the positions totally failed to represent rich meaningfulness of Buddha's silence and the philosophic situation that emerged went day by day, beyond the condition of repair. That is why Nāgārjuna took upon himself that it was his duty to show that both the positions are untenable as there is world of difference between what they convey on the one hand and what the Buddha intended to convey by his silence on the other. But, unfortunately, the most painful part of it is that, what the Buddha did not want to inculcate among the people for which he kept silence, was taken as the official position of the Buddha by his disciples and scholars. Buddha's official position was neither *Śūnyavāda* nor was it *sarvāstivāda*. Nāgārjuna did not wish any one of them to be taken as the official position of the Buddha either. In fact, Nāgārjuna is at pains to point out that he has no position to uphold. He openly says that he has nothing to put forth of his own. But that does not mean that he has nothing to say. Those who make frequent reference to his utterrances in the *Vigrahavyāvartani*[8] maintain that the *karikā* itself says that Nāgārjuna has no philosophical position at all to uphold and defend. Though number of scholars champion the view that he did not hold a philosophical position and that even if he had any, it involves a self-contradiction,[9] it appears that this view of theirs seems to have arisen out of their failure to properly grasp the point of Nāgārjuna. His contention that 'I have nothing (original) to expound' is so rich that it implies following points : a) First, whatever of significance is to be said is already said by the Buddha. That is why at the very outset of the treatise he bows to the Buddha and declares that he is carrying forward that work which the Buddha had already taken up in hand.[10] b) Second, what is said in *Madhyamakaśāstra* is simply an explication of Buddha's teaching. Though explication need not bring novelty in the thesis, such an exercise becomes unavoidable, for it is undertaken to restore Buddha's teaching to its legitimate status. More importantly, it is directed at clarifying confusions and misunderstanding about Budcha's teaching prevalent in the then existing intellectual atmosphere. (c) Thirdly, it means that although the resultant position is not a new one, it is nevertheless a respectable philosophical position. (d) Fourthly, being perhaps the first systematizer of Buddha's message, his job, as he conceives it, is to explicate Buddha's position as unambigiously as possible. This being the case, Nāgārjuna holds, and perhaps rightly, that he has nothing of his own to put forth. Being consistent with him Candrakīrti points out that *Mādhyamikas* need not adopt an independence method too[11] to make their point understandable. For, it is neither required nor is necessary. So no one should be under the impression that *Mādhyamikas* have no philosophical position at all to defend and uphold.

Here it is striking to note that it is the philosophical position expounded in the *Madhyamakaśāstra* that *Mādhyamikas* were initially aiming to uphold. But it is unfortunate that like the Buddha, they, too, fell a prey to misunderstanding, confusion and errors. The situation needs to be viewed in this way so that the so-called inner contradiction in Nāgārjuna's professy and practice, as it is alleged, will wither away. That is, his utterances like 'I have nothing to say' or 'I have no position at all' should not be taken in the strict literal sense so as to enable us to say that '*Mādhyamikas* have no position' is a wrong outlook entertained out of lack of proper understanding.

Madhyamā Pratipad : A Genuine mean between the two extreme positions

In this connection, the impact of the advocacy of *Śūnyavāda* as an official philosophy of the Buddha was too far to imagine. It mainly contributed to reject not only those objects which are not inhabitants of the world but also those objects which really constitute the world. Scholars and interpreters of Buddha's message, under the banner of proper interpretation of 'Buddha's silence' and of his not infrequent use of *Śūnyatā* come to deny ruthlessly the ontological status even to the genuinely real items of the world. Given this approach the kind of position that come to be ascribed to the Buddha and its important consequences have already been outlined earlier[12] and it is needless to indulge into the same exercise once more. Accordingly, we now take to highlight the other way of understanding the official position of the Buddha. This too, emerged out of interpretation of Buddha's silence on certain issues. Thus, *Sarvāstivāda* come to be understood as another version of the official position of the Buddha and that also led to the emergence of consequences which were alien to and at variance from what the Buddha wanted sincerely to uphold. The versions—literal *Śūnyavāda* and *Sarvastivāda*—that come to masquerade as rival interpretations of Buddha's philosophy are so one sided that they presented almost diagonally opposite frameworks and each of them was, in its characteristic way, a distortion of Buddha's position. It is the prevalence of these two warring positions which might have motivated Nāgārjuna to put forth real mean between the two through non-clinging to any one of them.[13] Thus, *Madhyamā Pratipad*, according to Nāgārjuna, is the official position of the Buddha and Buddhism and is to put it forth that he endeavoured to write the treatie called *Madhyamakaśāstra*.

As pointed out earlier, Buddha's silence on metaphysical issues was the main shaft around which the whole array of misinterpretation rotates. One of these is the realism of *Sarvāstivāda* which needs some clarifications. As *Mādhyamikas* like Nāgārjuna entered into a debate with adherents of *Śūnyavāda* so also they had to enter into confrontation with the view held by *Sarvāstivāda*. Were *Sarvāstivādins* to say that the objects which are part and parcel of the furniture of the world are real, *Mādhyamikas* would have had different reason to open a battle against them. But they upheld the view that not only objects which are genuinely there are existent but also the objects which we deem to there. Thus, according to them, even the objects which we imagine to be there or the objects which we perceive hallucinatorily are equally existent. Not only that, but according to them, concepts, notions, linguistic expressions, signs, symbols etc. which, in the strict sense of the term, are part of our communicational tool *i.e.*, language and to which we suppose to have no reference outside the language, too, are existent. This position of them led them to be known as *Sarvāstivādins*, that is, those who uphold that 'Sarvaṁ asti' *i.e.*, everything exists (*i.e.* table exists, the concept of table exists and the table which one sees in the dream equally exists.) This position further led them to maintain that our experience is itself sufficient to talk about the matters of fact. In *Sarvāstivāda*, thus, at least prima facie, an equation between experience and knowledge seems to have been accepted and an experience seems to have been taken to be both the necessary and sufficient condition of knowledge. Therefore, if the question is asked 'What is the gurantee to say that such and such is the case?' *Sarvāstivādin* would answer that our experience would suffice to warrant the information and our claim that such is the case. But allowing our experience to function as a gurantee-card in the realm of justificatory epistemology, towards the justifiability of our knowledge-claims, gives rise to the following difficulties : a) First of all, one will fail to make distinction between experience and knowledge. b) secondly, we will also fail to demarcate between facts and fictions c) Thirdly, so far our experience is concerned we cannot succeed in making distinction between veridical perception, illusion and hallucination and all of them will have to be treated on par with each other. d) Fourthly. if experience is considered to be the sole guarantee then there will be trouble on the count of validating experience—transcending knowledge claims. *Sarvāstivādins*, however, accepts all kinds of items to be real no matter how they are given. Restricting for the presents to items disclosed experientially it becomes extremely difficult to draw a distinction between that which is the object of normal perception and that which is an object of illusion or hallucination. But in so far as this is the case it will lead us to accept pseudo and quasi-real entities, too, as part and parcel of the furniture of the world. Taking in this way all sorts of objects to be real leads to creation of an ontological slum. Disagreeing with this picture of the world one may hold that these things are real—but real on different strata. But this modification in the *Sarvāstivādin's* picture of the world is not free from difficulties either. For, we will have then to accept the world to be a multistoreyed building and we will have to envisage a system of either ascending or descending order of objectivity with the proviso that as we climb up or down this multistoreyed world there will be corresponding rise or fall in the reality of a thing. If, on the contrary, we are unwilling to admit the world to be a multistoreyed complex, the only alternative left to be considered is that of the other world. That is, *Sarvāstivādins* may say that if some objects do not exist in this word then they must be subsisting elsewhere, possibly in the other world. But this analysis is also not free from errors, for, it unnecessarily implies the multiplication of worlds. Moreover, platonistic realism of *Sarvās-tivāda* does not stop here. In addition to its earlier analysis it further maintains that our linguistic expressions are such that they refer to things outside and thus expressions and things for which they are expressioas stand in one—one relation—with each other. Thus, according to *Sarvāstivādins,* our language becomes descriptive of the world. So, if the question is asked : 'What kind of world would be there ?' they would answer that kind of world should be there which would be reflected through our language and the kind of world which is grasped in fand through the language alone can be said to be satisfactorily knowable. That means according to platonistic realism of *Sarvāstivāda,* there are only those items in the world which have some counter-part in our linguistic frame. It **further** implies that there are as many objects in the world as linguistic expressions are. Thus, this analysis of *Sarvāstivādins* about word-world relation compels us to accept such items which are held to be there due to the conceptual and linguistic play. For instance, *Sarvāstivādins* will have to provide a room to square-circles, unicons or the son of a barren woman.

It is against such a disastrous platonistic world view of *Sarvās-tivādins* that *Mādhyamikas* in general and Nāgārjuna in particular, had to open a confrontation to show that *Sarvāstivādins* have totally misunderstood the Buddha and the philosophic position which they attempted to put forth as a philosophy of the Buddha may be anything but Buddha's philosophy. Thus, in the eyes of Nāgārjuna both, the *Śūnyavādins* who held that nothing is real and *Sarvāstivādins* who held that anything is real, distort and misrepresent the philosophic position of the Buddha.

Addressing both of them Nāgārjuna says that the Buddha has denied both the extremes.[14] For, the latter confers ontological status on those items which are not genuinely real, while the former deprives even genuinely real items from their ontologicality. Candrakīrti commenting on the *kārika* says that not all items are real but only those items which are given to us in and through properly understood *Pratītyasamutpāda* alone are real. Likewise not all items are unreal but those items which are not given through such *Pratītya Samutpāda* are unreal. Thus, the smallest common denominator of these two positions is that some items are real. This real mean between the two extreme ontological positions is called *Madhyamāpratipad*.[15] *Mādhyamika* school of Buddhism, alone, gives due respects to the real inhabitants of the world and thereby comprehends the genuine nature of the world as it is constituted and structured through the doctrine of *Pratītya Samutpāda* properly understood. This it does by adopting a proper perspective towards the nature of the world—viz. *Nirvāṇa* which reveals the unreality of unreal items—and employing a methodological tool—viz. *Śūnyatā*-to do away the otherwise proliferative ontology, misleading epistemology and defective linguistic frame. Each one of them is extremely important in our coming to develop the philosophical position under consideration. Such a school of philosophy—*Mādhyamika*—is free from conflicting extreme philosophical positions like realism or nihilism[16] Candrakīrti further contends that so far as the commonsensical attempt of understanding the nature of the world and its structure are concerned, layman is likely to get considerably confused by such extreme view-points. It is for these people, who peep into the deep structure of the world out of curiosity, that Nāgārjuna comes to explain, elaborate and clarify *Madhyamā Pratipad*, a true philosophy, reflecting the nature of the world by doing away the impact of dual extreme philosophic positions.[17]

The extended version of extreme realism and nihilism is its application in the field of Psychology—leading to acceptance of *Self* and denial of Self respectively. Of these, realists contend that the self is unchanging substratum behind all the activities. It is the basis of moral and religious activities and it has important connection in the act of knowing. For, if it is not admitted as a real item, then no knowledge is possible. This being the case, self is there. Nihilists, on the contrary, hold the view that there is no such a thing as the self. It cannot be regarded as the substratum behind all the activities, since it just does not exist. These two positions of realists and nihilists come to be known as *ātmavāda* and *anātmavāda* respectively. These were not only held by Pre-mādhyamika schools of Buddhism which Nāgārjuna criticises, but similar trend was also in vogue in the non-Buddhist world of philosophy. Candrakīrti takes recourse of some such views expressed by *Sānkhya* and *Lokāyata* schools[18] which were automatically criticised as they differ from Buddha's teaching and also *Mādhyamika* standpoint. Nāgārjuna says that Buddha had never taught anybody anywhere that there is *ātmā* or that there is *anātmā*.[19] To hold, irrespective of Buddha's teaching that there is *ātmā* and explain the modes of behaviour with the help of it gives rise to one extreme.[20] Likewise, to regard that there is no *ātmā* and explain the behaviour of things, entities and individuals purely mechanistically leads to another equally troublesome extreme position.[21] On this issue, Candrakirti clarifies that we are not nihilists as is sometimes said, nor, too, are we realists as it is commonly told. Rather we are the true followers of the teaching of the Buddha. We uphold the view which at once avoids the controversy between total existence and utter non-existence, for both the positions are untenable.[22] Philosophically speaking, there is no action, doer of action or fruit of action etc., for, all of them are unreal.[23] Therefore, irrespective of it, to hold that they are there is as good as to accept mirage or city of *gandharvas* to be there.[24] This being the case, it is, we, the Mādhy-amikas, who uphold the reality of those items which are genuinely real (*svābhāvika*) and do not embrace conflicting positions such as eternalism or annihilationism.[25] It is *Madhyamā Pratipad* which strikes the real mean between the two as its upholders do not know whether there is some such thing called '*ātmā*' or not. Such a middle position between the two extreme poles is beyond the reach of description.[26] It can only be comprehended, cognized, followed, and practised. There are implications of the middle position in social, moral, religious, epistemological fields of inquiry as well. But they need not destract us here. For the present it suffices to note that *Madhyamā Pratipad*, true philosophy of the Buddha explicated at the hands of Nāgārjuna, is a real mean between the two extreme positions held by *Śūnyavādins* and *Sarvāstivādins*.

The Connection of *Madhyamā Pratipad* with *Pratītya Samutpāda, Śūnyatā and Nirvāṇa*

Earlier we pointed out that *Madhyamā pratipad*—the philoso-phical position of Nāgārjuna—rests on its three pillars—viz. *Pratītyasamutpāda, Śūnyatā* and *Nirvāṇa*. Of these, first two viz. *Pratītyasamutpāda* and *Śūnyatā* are directly connected with his philosophical position—*Madhyamāpratipad*, while *Nirvāṇa* is conn-ected with it in a different way. Let us see, how these pillars of Nāgārjuna's philosophical structure hold the weight of Nāgārjuna's philosophical position—viz. *Madhyamāpratipad*.

Madhyamā Pratipad and Pratītya Samutpāda

In the *karika* 18 of 24th chapter of his treatise—*Madhyama-kaśastra* Nāgārjuna comes to interlink *Pratītyasamutpāda, śūnyatā* and *Madhyamāpratipad* saying that all of them give rise to the same philosophical position. That is, they variantly contribute to the emergence of the same important philosophical position. What is given in and through *Pratītyasamutpāda* is also revealed through the the employment of *śūnyatā* and what is revealed through *śūnyatā* is comprehended as philosophy of *Madhyamā Pratipad*. It means that *Pratītyasamutpada* and *śūnyatā* give rise to the same philoso-phical position—*Madhyamā Pratipad* but via different routes and thus converge upon the same world.

Pratītyasamutpada gives us an understanding about the nature of the world. But there are two ways of understanding of *Pratītya-*

samutpāda. Commonsensical understanding of *Pratītyasamutpāda* leads us to comprehend that it is a causal theory explaining the emergence of the things in the world. On this view things are casually connected with one another. Rightly understood *Pratītya-samutpāda,* on the contrary, reveals that we cannot hope to maintain any type of necessary connection between or among the things which are presented unto us in sequential form. Nāgārjuna puts forth *Pratītyasamutpāda* in the latter sense, as a theory designed to give the nature, structure and constitution of the world alongwith the things in it, and as the Buddha wanted us to understand, which of course, removes at once, the normal and prevalent misunderstanding about the nature of the world cherished by either the layman or/and misguided philosopher, no matter whether he hails from Buddhist or non-Buddhist camp. Thus, rightly understood *Pratītyasamutpāda* gives rise to *Madhyamāpratipad* in two ways : a) that it leads to hold a middle position between 1) that things in the world as they are presented one after the other, are causally connected, and 2) that things in ihe world are not causally connected. The real mean—*madhyama mārga*—between the two is that the things which are given to us, are given one after the other. Though it gives rise to an impression of a sequence, yet things can merely be said to be connected with one another. It does not give us consequence but merely sequence among the things. (b) *Pratītya Samutpāda,* likewise, gives us a middle between two features of the world viz. change and continuity. That is it leads to hold that change is the basic feature and continuity as the functional feature of the world is one extreme and to hold that continuity is basic and change is merely resultant feature of the world is another extreme. It is a real mean between the two to hold that change as well as continuity constitute the real nature of the world. This does not, however, mean that eternal things undergo change. They could be short-lived. Thus on the count of the connection between rightly understood *Pratitya Samutpāda* and *Madhyamā Pratipad* we find that both of them converge upon the proper understanding of the nature of the world alongwith the things inhabiting it. Thus, *Madhyamā Pratipad* is not a speculative theory about the world but rather a warrantable compromise between the extreme positions and warring camps.

Another point of their connection is that *Pratītyasamutpāda* and *Madhyamāpratipad* converge upon the same world view exhibiting the same feature of the world. We already pointed out the eight important characteristic features of *Partītyasamutpāda*. Here we throw light on those characteristic features which are commonly held as features of both *Pratītyasamutpāda* and *Madhyamāpratipad*.[27]

(i) *Anekārtham* : *Madhyamā pratipad* as a true characterisation of Buddha's philosophy is an expression having repurcussions on more than one fields of knowledge. In ontology it is a mean between existence and non-existence. In psychology it is a mean between *ātmavāda* and *anātmavāda*. In morality it is a mean between self mortification and excessive enjoyment. In epistemology it is a mean between two positions viz. every knowledge claim is certifiable and no knowledge claim is certifiable and so on. In the light of such multitude of implications of *Madhyamāpratipad* it is indeed *anekārtha*.

(ii) *Anānārtham* : Though *Madhyamāpratipad* has implications in various fields, yet common thread which runs though all of them is the same—not to cling either to this that extreme. Thus, inspite of varied applications of *Madhyamāpratipad*, it does not give us different world perspectives. In so far as it gives rise to a unitory world-view, it is called *anānārtha i.e., abhinnārtha*.

(iii) *Anucchedam* : We saw that *Madhyamāpratipad* as a philosophical position arises when we understand *Pratītyasamutpāda* rightly, adopt a proper philosophical focus—*Nirvāṇa* and use a methodological tool *Śūnyatā* to comprehend the real nature of the world. But even though one adopts *Madhyamāpratipad* in the way in which the Bundha wants us to adopt, the fact remains that those who do not follow *Madhyamāpratipad* in this way, remain under the sway of misunderstanding, confusion and errors. As there is a permanent possibility of such a misunderstanding being removed through *Madhyamāpratipad* and since once adopted it continues to prevail, it is called annucchedaṁ.

(iv) *Aśāśvatam* : This characteristic feature of *Madhyāmā pratipad* can be understood thus : a) *Madhyamāpratipad* as a philosophical position of the Buddha and also of Nāgārjuna need to be comprehended in this way. But in so far as we remain under the sway of its wrong interpretation, we do not come to develop a right understanding about it. But that does not mean that rightful understanding of it will just never dawn upon us. In other words, it means that improper understanding of *Madhyamāpratipad* is a contingent feature and there is every possibility of doing away with it. Therefore, it is called *aśāśvata*. b) Secondly, like *Nirvāṇa* as a philosophical perspective, *Madhyamāpratipad* as a philosophical position, too, needs to be developed by a person. A person who develops it, understands the nature of the world properly. His understanding of *Madhyamāpratipad* will last so long as he is alive and it cannot be transmitted readymade to another person. As a development of such a philosophical position is not a transferable property, it becomes nul and void as soon as a death of a person takes place. Therefore, it is characterised as *aśāśvata*.

Madhyamā Pratipad And Śūnyatā

Now, if *Pratītyasamutpāda* and *Madhyamāpratipad*, *Pratityasamatpada* and *śūnyatā* are intimately connected, then there is no wonder in saying that *Madhyamāpratipad* and *Śūnyatā* are also connected with each other. We have already seen how *Pratītyasamutpāda* is connected with *Madhyamāpratipad*. It now remains to see how *Śūnyatā* can be said to be related with *Madhyamāpratipad* which leads to the advocacy of a real mean between the two positions.

It is argued that *Śūnyatā* as a methodologieal tool is wielded by Nāgārjuna with a view to point out unreality of unreal objects and thereby demolish the otherwise ontological slum leading to improper comprehension. Ontologically understood, *Śūnyatā* reveals the middle position as it counts only those items which are given through rightly understood *Pratītyasamutpāda*. It is thus a mean between the two positions : i) that all items are real and ii) no item is real. Nāgārjuna tells us, with the help of *Śūnyatā*, to take only those items to be real which are genuinely there.

Methodologically *Śūnyatā* is used as a censor of *dharma*, *padārtha* and *bhāva*. With regard to *dharmas* it tells us that their shareability is no guarantee or their reality. We are not told that there are no *dharmas*. Nor are we told that all *dharmas* are real. It only says that those *dharmas* which are expressed through language may be and often are unreal. In fact it leads to the middle position between : i) all dharmas are real and ii) no dharma is real.

When it comes to the states of things Candrakīrti maintains that we never say that all states of things (bhāvas) are unreal—*niḥsvābhāvika*. On the contrary, we say that those states which are derivative alone are *niḥsvābhāvika*. However, if there is any state of a thing which is structural or unrelative then such a state of a thing can rightly be said to be real. This is, how, again. this phase of *Śūnyatā* reveals a mean between two positions viz. i) that all states of things are real and ii) no states of thing is real. It tells us that those states of things which are *svābhāvika* alone are real. Therefore, Nāgārjuna warns us that those who take all states of things to be real or unreal fail to comprehend the nature of the things and thereby do not understand what is proper.[28]

On the issue of language, Nāgārjuna, no doubt, seems to be more critical. But his lookout is not pessimistic. There, too, he seems to have followed the mean between the two positions. For, he never says that any language is inappropriate. He, rather, says, that our ordinary language is prone to create more problems than it solves. We hope to use it with utmost caution and care with a view to avoid extremists position and adopt a middle one. A note of caution sounded by Nāgārjuna wants to avoid the extremes : i) that any language is useful and appropriately descriptive and ii) that not a single language is useful. We should, rather, use that language or available language in such a way that it brings out the nature of uniquely particular and discrete items without disturbing thir nature.

Madhyamā Pratipad and Nirvāṇa

Uptil now, we saw the connection between *Madhyamāpratipad*— a philosophical position—with *Pratītyasamutpāda* and *Śūyatā*—two pillars of Nāgārjuna's philosophy. *Nirvāṇa*—one more pillar of the same philosophical structure—is also intimately connected with *Madhyamā Pratipad Nirvāṇa* gets altogether novel treatment at the hands of Nāgārjuna when he, differing from traditional outlook about it, gives a novel interpretation, as a philosophical focus that is at once connected with the world and philosophical position. Through adoption of *Nirvāṇa* as a proper perspective one comes to develop an insight into the deep structure of the world as it is constituted and thereby comes to understand that there are only some items which can be said to be genuinely real and are philoso- phically interesting. But more seriously one feels the unreality of unreal items which in normal course of understanding are taken to be real and part and parcel of the furniture of the world. The pressure of the reality of unreal things on the one hand an urge to develop a proper world view on the other hand make one wield a methodological tool—*Śūnyatā* to do away with the troublesome platonistic world view. Thus, adoption of proper perspective is, through *Pratītyasamutpāda* and *Śūnyatā*, instrumental to comprehension of true philosophical position—viz. *Madhyamā pratipad*. But, again a person does not come to subscribe to the philosophy of the Buddha-*Madhyamāpratipad* unless he comes to do away with the warring extremes and adopts the proper philosophical perspective—*Nirvāṇa*.[29] Thus *Madhyamāpratipad* and *Nirvāṇa* are reciprocally connected with each other, in the sense that without Nirvāṇa *Madhyamāpratipad* is impossible and without *Madhyamāpratipad Nirvāṇa* is meaningless.[30]

General Implications of Madhyamā Pratipad

Mādhyamika philosophy can by no mean be taken to be easily understood if anybody fails to comprehend the import of *Pratītyasamutpāda*, *Śūnyatā* and *Nirvāṇa*, the way in which Nāgārjuna and his commentator expound it. Why is the school called *madhyamaka* and its followers as Mādhyamika ?[31]   To be true to its name, it refers to the objective *madhyamā* i.e. middle between two positions, which teaches us to follow it. More importantly, it teaches us to avoid inclination to any extreme position arising on whichever level. The middle way, thus, amounts to avoidance of any extreme position, however attractive it might be. If this be the fundamental teaching of Buddhism and of the Buddha and if all Buddhists subscribe to it then they should be called *Mādhyamikas*.[32] But the discussion on the matter under consideration shows that, irrespective of the intended version of Buddha's silence, people erroneously characterise his teaching as realistic or monistic and what not. No wonder that they cease to be *Mādhyamikas*. Nāgārjuna, a true follower of the Buddha, systematically examines these views, particularly on the issues of ontological matters overcomes the finality of being and meaninglessness of non being.[33] He is equally critical of the warring issues of existence—non-existence, real—unreal etc. *Madhyamāpratipad* understood in this way as a true mean between bi-polarised philosophical positions has always implications of fundamental import which may find echoes in individual as well as social l, moral and religious life. But *Madhyamāpratipad* has also important implications in epistemology, methodology and such other spheres of human inquiry. Whether in ontology, epistemology or elsewhere it seeks to avoid extremism of any sort, instrumental to misunderstanding and error. *Madhyamāpratipad* is not an advocacy of an inttellectual coward who does not wish to risk examination and enquiry. It is rather a position of the one who, being convinced of phisophical unserviceability of subscription to any extremist position and on the basis of honest inquiry, wants to avoid such extremes whichever sphere of human knowledge and endeavour they might be attracting our attention.

Total organic connectedness and utter discreteness of the world, or eternalism and annihilationism are such extended and extremist versions of philosophical positions. Whatever the initial and prima facie attractiveness of such positions, on closer scrutiny and deeper inquiry they are seen to present such formidable difficulties that the positions under consideration turn out to be uninteresting and untenable. Instead of being trapped by them Nāgārjuna, following the Buddha, wants to avoid them and instead wants to adopt philosophical position of *Madhyamāpratipad*—the middle way. One finds this to be the general theme of the culture of Indian origin and may be rightly regarded to be the contribution of Buddhism in general and Nāgārjuna in particular.

It was not only in the intellectual side of human life—individual as well as social—that Buddha's message was misinterpreted and distortorted after his demise but also in practical aspect of human life—particularly man's moral and religious life, both individual and social. Buddha's teaching of not to do many things which are against social interest were wrongly taken to mean that Buddha himself does not seem to be happy about practical life. Consequently, interpretation of Buddha's message gave rise to ascecticism of an extreme kind. Likewise on the issue of liberation and emancipation of self from worldly activities undue importance was given to self-mortification and it was taken to be official view of the Buddha. Materialism on the other hand, advocated, that, one does not know, what is the fate of self after the death and hence it is futile and in vain to go in for liberation of self. Instead it is better and advisable to enjoy the life as much as possible. Moral and religious practices, social relationship, modes of fellowship etc. were in the same vain considered in diametrically different ways. On the one hand it was claimed that moral, religious and other modes of action and behaviour must be followed to the letter both in individual and social life come what may, and without any alteration and modification, however pressing and justifiable the need to do so. On the other hand it was that in the absence of specific guidance from the Buddha one is free to chose that mode of moral and religious practice that is beneficial—individually and socially. Thus, moral or religious practices, modes of fellowship or social relationship were either considered in utter rigid and inflexible way or so relativistically that ordinary person must have been totally baffled and confused. The anarchy and chaos that obtained in intellec tual and social life demanded systematization of Buddha's teaching insuch a way that it will not be at variance from Buddha's teaching on the one hand and, on the other, will ensure proper understanding on our part. For, without such a kind of proper understanding consideration of its applicability to and implications in practical life is a futile exercise. It is in this situation that Nāgārjuna took upon himself the task of systematization of the intellectual aspect of Buddha's teaching and as a result of his prolonged enquiry put forth *Madhyamāpratipad* to be the official position of the Buddha, anchored at once in *Pratītyaramutpāda Śūnyatā* and *Nirvāṇa* and seeking to avoid any extremist position, however attractive it may be. This is the singular and memorable achievement of Nāgārjuna and, as remarked earlier, it has left quite deep foot prints on our cultural heritage. That is its greatness and importance. But it also needs to be understood that its framework cannot be understood in the absence of *Pratītyasamutpāda Śūnyatā* and *Nirvāṇa*. Nor does any of them have that significance, which they have, bereft of their interconnection with *Madhyamāpratipad*. It is to articulate this framework of Nāgārjuna's philosophy was our task in the present work and to what extent we have succeeded in accomplishing it be better left to the judgement of sensitive readers.

NOTES

1. Garbe, R., 'Sankhya' ERE, Vol. XI, pp. 190-91. also Smart
   N., Indian Philosophy, Encylopaedia of Philosophy, Vol. IV,
   pp. 155-168.

2. Smart, N., 'Indian Philosophy', Encyclopaedia of Philosophy, Vol. IV, pp. 155-168.

3. Sinha, J., *A History of Indian Philosophy*, Vol. I, pp. 581, 593, 594.

4. Matilal, B.K., "Ontological problem in Nyāya, Buddhism and Jainism" (JIP) Vol. V, No. 1-2, p. 92.

5. Chapter I, p. 2.

6. Murti, T.R,V., '*The Central Philosophy of Buddhism.*' p. 52.

7. *Ibid*, p. 217 (cf.) Ketkar B.G., Nāgārjuna : a fresh study, p. 75.

8. *Vigrahavyāvartani*, 29.

9. May, J., "On Madhyamika Philosophy" (JIP) Vol. 6 No. 3, p. 234.

10. *Madhyamakaśāstra* 1.2

   Yaḥ pratītyasamutpādaṁ prapañcopaśamaṁ śivaṁ/desayāmāsa saṁbuddhaṁ taṁ vande vadatāṁ varaṁ/

11. *Prasannapadā*, Na ca mādhyamikasya sataḥ Svatantramanumānaṁ kartuṁ yuktaṁ p. 5.

12. Chapter III, pp.

13. May, J., "On Madhyamika Philosophy" (JIP) Vol. 6 No. 3, p. 233.

14. *Madhyamakaśārtra*; 15.7.

   Kātyāyanāvavādeca asti nāstīti cobhayaṁ/pratiṣiddhaṁ bhagavatā bhāvābhāvavibhāvinā

15. *Prasannapadā*, Yadenayorantayormadhyaṁ . . . iyamucyate kāsyapa madhyamā pratipad. p. 118.

16. *Ibid*, Tadevaṁ madhyamakadarśane astitva . . . / p. 120.

17. *Ibid*; mumukṣubhiḥ etat darśanadvaya nirāsena bhāvanīya p. 121.

18. *Ibid* ; Ātmetyapi prajñapitam sānkhyādibhiḥ, anatmetyapi prajñapitaṁ lokāyatikaiḥ p. 153.

19. *Madhyamakaśāstra*; 18.6

   Ātmetyapi prajñapitamanātmetyapi deśitaṁ/Buddhair ātmā na cānātmā kaścidityapi desitaṁ/

20. *Prasannapad*ā; Ātmeti kaśyapa ayameko'ntaḥ/p. 153.

21. *Ibid*, Nairātmyamityayaṁ dvitīyo'ntaḥ/p. 153.

22. *Ibid*, Na vayaṁ nāstikāḥ/astitvanāstitvadvaya vādanirāsena. . . vidyotayāmaḥ p. 142.

23. *Ibid*, Na ca karmakartṛphalādikaṁ nāstīti brumaḥ . . .vyavasthāpayāmaḥ p. 142.

24. *Ibi*d, Ta ete . . . niḥsvabhāvāḥ veditavyāḥ p. 143.

25. *Ibid*, Tasmānmādhyamikānāmeva . . . darsanadvaya prasaṅgo nāstīti vijñeyaṁ p. 143.

26. *Ibid*, Yadetadanayorantayoramadhyaṁ tadarūpyaṁ madhyamā pratipad . . . p. 153.

27. Compare kāriḳās 1.1 and 18.11 respectively. Anirodamanutpādamanucchedamaśāśvataṁ/anekārthamānānarthamʼanāgamamanirgamaṁ/

            And

Anekārthamanārthamanucchedamaśāśvataṁ   etattalokanāthānāṁ buddhānāṁ śāsanāmṛtaṁ/

28. *Madhyamakaśastra* 5.8,

Astitvaṁ ye tu paśyanti nāstitvaṁ cālpabuddhyaḥ/bhāvānāṁ te na paśyanti dṛṣṭavyo paśamaṁśivaṁ

29. *Prasannapad*ā; astitvanāstitva dvayavādanirāsena . . . vidyotayāmaḥ p. 142.

30. *Ratnā*vali; 1.42 Bhāvābhāvaparamaśakṣayo nirvāṇamucyate

31. *Madhyamakaś*āstra, Introduction, p. ix.

32. May J., "On Madhyamika Philosophy" (JIP), Vol. No. 6, No. 3, p. 233.

33. Sprung M., *The Lucid Exposition of the Middle Way*, p. 23.

BIBLIOGRAPHY

1. Bapat, P. V., *2500 Years of Buddhism*, Director, Publications Division, Ministry of Information and Broadcasting, Delhi, 1956.

2. Barua, B. M., *Prolegomena to History of Buddhist, Philosophy*, Calcutta University Press, Calcutta, 1918.

3. Barlingay, S. S., "The Significance of Pratītya Samutpāda, Sāmānyalaksaṇa and Apoha in Buddhism", Buddha Jayanti Lecture, XLV Session, Indian Philosophical Congress, Osmania University, Hyderabad, 1971.

4. Bharatiya, M. C., *Causation in Indian Philosophy*, Vimal Prakashan, Ghaziabad, (U. P.) 1973.

5. Bhattacharya, K., "Does, Śūnyatā mean Nothingness?—Reply to Prof. Ketkar's Objection" *Journal of Philosophical Association*; Vol. VIII No. 29-30, 1961.

6. Bhattacharya, K., "The Concept of Śūnyatā—An Analysis of Nāgārjuna's Philosophy", *Journal of Philosophical Association*, Vol. VII, No. 28, 1960.

7. Bhikkhu, J. Kashyap (ed.); *Anguttara Nikāya*; Nalanda Devanagari Pali Series, Vol. IV, Pali Publication Board, (Bihar Govt.), 1960.

8. Bhikkhu J. Kashyap (ed.), *Dīgha Nikāya*; Nalanda Devanagari Series, Vol. IV, Pali Publication Board, (Bihar Govt.), 1958.

9. Bhikkhu J. Kashyap (ed.), *Majjimā Nikāya*, Nalanda Devanagari Pali Series, Pali Pali Publication Board (Bihar Govt.), 1958.

10. Carnap, R., *Philosophy of Rudolf Carnap*, Schilpp, P. A. (ed); The Library of Living Philosophies, Vol. XI, Cambridge University Press, London, 1963.

11. Candrakīrti, *Prasannapadā*; Vaidya, P. L. (ed.) Bauddha Sanskrit Text No. 10, Mithila Institute, Darbhanga, 1960.

12. Conze, E., *Buddhist Thought in India*, George Allen and Unwin Ltd., London, 1962.

13. Dahlke, P., *Buddhist Essays* Bhikkhu Sīlācāra (ed.), Mac Millan and Co., London, 1908.

14. Dange, (Mrs.) S. S., *Bauddha Dharma āṇi Talvajnāna*, For, Maharashtra Vidpapeetha Grantha Nirmiti Mandal, Continental Prakashan, Pune, 1980.

15. Dasgupta, S. N., *A History of Indian Philosophy*, 5 Vols., Cambridge University Press, London, 1957.

16. Datta N., *Mahāyāna Buddhism*, Motilal Banarasīdas, Delhi, 1977.

17. Davids, (Mrs.) Rhys., "Paticca Samutpāda", *Encyclopaedia of Religion and Ethics*, Vol. IV.

18. Garbe, R., "Sānkhya", *Encyclopaedia of Religion and Ethics*, Vol. XI.

19. Grimm, G., *The Doctrine of the Buddha*, Offizen W. Drugulin, Leipzig, 1926.

20. Gupta, R., "Twelve Membered Dependent Origination—An Attempted Re-appraisal" *Journal of Indian Philosophy*, Vol. V No. 1, 1977.

21. Hall, R., "Monism and Pluralism" *Encyclopaedia of Philosophy*, Edward, P. (ed.), Vol. V.

22. Hiriyanna, M., *Outline of Indian Philosophy*, George Allen and Unwin Ltd., Bombay, 1973.

23. Hume, D., *Treatise of Human Nature*, J. M. Dent and Sons Ltd., New York, 1974.

24. Humphrey, C., *Studies in the Middle Way*, George Allen and Unwin Ltd., London, (3rd edn), 1959.

25. Inada, K. K., "Some Basic Misconceptions of Buddhism", *International Philosophical Quarterly* Vol. IX, No. 1, 1969.

26. Ingalls, D. D. H., "Samkara's Argument Against Buddhist", *Philosophy East-West,* Vol. III No. 4, 1954.

27. Jayatilleke, K. N., *Early Buddhist Theory of Knowledge*, George Allen and Unwin Ltd., London, 1963.

28. Jones, R. F., 'Mysticism', *Encyclopaedia of Religion and Ethics*, Vol. IX.

29. Joshi, G. N., *Ātman and Moksa*, Gujarat University Press, Ahmedabad, 1965.

30. Jung, J. W., "Emptiness", *Journal of Indian Philosophy*, Vol. II, No. 1, 1972.

31. Jung, J.W., "The Problem of the Absolute in the Madhyamika School". *Journal of Indian Philosophy*, Vol. II, No. 1, 1972

32. Kalupahana, D., *Buddhist Philosophy—A Historical Analysis*, An East-West Centre Book, The University Press of Hawai, Honolulu, 1966.

33. Keith, A. B., *Buddhist Philosophy in Indian and Ceylon* Chaukhamba Sanskrit Series XXVI Varanasi, 1963.

34. Kern, H., *Mannual of Indian Buddhism* (Encydopaedia of Indo-Aryan Research).

35. Ketkar, B. C., "Does Śūnyatā Mean Nothingness?" *Journal of Philosophical Association* Vol. VIII No. 29-30, 1961.

36. Ketkar, B. G.' *Nāgārjuna : A Fresh Study*, (Ph. D. Thesis), Poona University, 1977 (Unpublished).

37. Mackie, J. L., *Cement of the Universe*, Clarendon Press, Oxford, 1974.

38. Marathe, M. P., "Nāgārjuna and Candrakīrti on Śūnyatā", *Indian Philosophical Quarterly*, Vol. VII No. 4, 1980.

39. Matilal, B. K., "Ontological Problems in Nyāya, Buddhism and Jainism—A Comparative Analysis", *Journal of Indian Philosophy*, Vol. VI No. 1, 1977.

40. May J., "On Mādhyamika Philosophy", *Journal of Indian Philosophy*, Vol. V No. 1, 1977.

41. Mitchell, W.D., "Buddhist Theories of Causation – A Commentary" *Philosophy East-West*, Vol. XXX No. 1, 1975.

42. Monier, W., *Buddhism*, Chaukhamba Sanskrit Series Office, Varanasi, (2nd edn.), 1964.

43. Mookherji, S., *Buddhist Philosophy of Universal Flux*, Motilal Banarasidas, Delhi, (2nd edn.), 1975.

44. Mukhopadhyaya, S., *Bauddhadarśanabinduḥ*, Sanskrit Vishvavidyalaya, Varanasi, Saṅvata 2021.

45. Murti, T.R.V., *The Central Philosophy of Buddhism*, George Allen and Unwin Ltd., London, (2nd edn.), 1968.

46. Nāgārjuna, *Madhyamakaśāstra*, Vaidya P. L. (ed.), Buddhist-Sanskrit Text No. 10; Mithila Institute, Darbhanga, 1960.

47. Nāgārjuna, *Ratnāvali*, Vaidya, P.L. (ed.), Buddhist Sanskrlt Text No. 10. Mithila Institute, Darbhanga, 1960.

48. Nāgārjuna, *Vigrahavyāvartani*, Vaidya, P.L. (ed.), Buddhist Sanskrit Text No. 10, Mithila Institute, Darbhanga, 1960.

49. Narain, H., "Śūnyavāda", *Philosophy East-West*, Vol. XIII No. 4, 1963.

50. Nayak, G. C., "The Mādhyamika Attack on Essentialism—A Critical Appraisal', *Philosophy East-West*, Vol. XXIX No. 4, 1979.

51. Pande, G. C.. *Studies in the Origins of Buddhism*, Ancient History Research Series 1, University of Allahabad, Allahabad, 1957.

52. Pandeya, R.C. (ed.), *Buddhist Studies in India*, Motilal Banarasidas, Delhi, 1975.

53. Pandeya, R. C., "Mādhyamika Philosophy—A New Approach", *Philosophy Easl-West*, Vol. XIV No. 1, 1964.

54. Poussin, La De. V., "Mādhyamikas", *Encyclopaedia of Religion and Ethics*, Vol. VIII.

55. Poussin, La. De. V., "Nirvāṇa (Buddhist)", *Encyclopaedia of Religion and Ethics*, Vol. IX.

56. Poussin, La. De. V., "Philosophy (Buddhist)", *Encyclopaedia of Religion and Eihics*, Vol. IX.

57. Pratap Chandra, *Metaphysics of Perpetual Change*, Somayya Publication Pvt. Ltd., Bombay, 1978.

58. Promsen, P.S., *A Study of the Doctrine of Paticca Samutpāda in Theravāda*, (Ph.D. Thesis), Banaras Hindu University, Varanasi, (unpublished).

59. Pye, M., *Skilful Means*, Duck-worth and Co, London, 1978.

60. Radhakrishnan, S., (ed.), *History of Philosophy (Eastern and Western)*, George Allen and Unwin Ltd., London, (3rd imp.) 1967.

61. Radhakrishdan, S., *Indian Philosophy*, 2 Vols., George Allen and Unwin Ltd., London (10th imp.), 1977.

62. Robinson, R. H., "Some Logical Aspects of Nāgārjuna's Philosophy", *Philosophy East-West* Vol. VI, No. 4, 1957.

63. Ruegg, S. D., "The Uses of the Four Positions of The Catuskoti and The Problem of the Description of Reality in Mahāyāna Buddhism", *Journal of Indian Philosophy*, Vol. V No. 1, 1977.

64. Rupp, G., "The Relation Between Nirvāṇa and Saṁsāra", *Philosophy East-West*. Vol. XXI, No. 1, 1971.

65. Russell, B., *Our Knowledge of the External World*, George Allen and Unwin Ltd., London, 1972.

66. Russell, B., *Mysticism and Logic*, George Allen and Unwin Ltd., London (11th imp.), 1959.

67. Saṁkarācārya; *Brahmasūtra Bhāṣya*, Motilal Banarasidas, Delhi, 1964.

68. Sinha, J., *A History of Indian Philosophy*, Sinha Publishing House, Calcutta, 1956.

69. Smart, N., "Indian Philosophy", *Encyclapaedia of Philosophy*, Edward, P. (ed.) Vol. IV.

70. Sogen. Y., *Systems of Buddhistic Thought*, University of Calcutta, Calcutta, 1912.

71. Sprung, M., *The Lucid Exposition of the Middle Way*, Routledge and Kegan Paul, London, 1979.

72. Sprung M., (ed.); *The Problem of Two Truths in Buddhism and Vedānta*, D. Reidel Publishing Company, Holland, 1973.

73. Stanley, R., *Nihilism*, Yale University Press, London, 1969.

74. Stcherbatsky, T., *Buddhist Logic*, 2 vols., Dover Publication, Inc., New York, 1962.

75. Stcherbatsky T., [*Central Conception of Buddhism*, Motilal Banarasidas, Varanasi, 1974.

76. Stcherbatsky, T., *The Conception of Buddhist Nirvāṇa*, Motilal Banarasidas, Varanasi, (2nd edn.), 1977.

77. Suzuki, D. T., *The Essence of Buddhism*, The Buddhist Society, London (2nd edn.), 1947.

78. Suzuki, D. T., *Outline of Mahāyāna Buddhism*, Schocken Books, New York, (4th edn.), 1970.

79. Takakusu., J., *Essentials of Budhist Philosophy* Asia Publishing House, Bombay, (2nd edn.), 1956.

80. Tamura, K., "Some Developments of Buddhist Approach to Reality", *International Philosophical Quarterly*, Vol. IV, No. 4, 1964.

81. Thomas, E. J., *History of Buddhist Thought*, Routledge and Kegan Paul, London, (2nd edn.), 1951.

82. Trivedi, B. P., *An Examination of the Concept of Change with Reference to Philosophies of Bergson and Buddhism* (Ph.D. Thesis), Poona University, (unpublished).

83. Upadhyaya, B., *Baudha darśana Mimāsṁsā*, Chaukhamba Vidya Bhavan, Varanasi, (2nd edn.), 1954.

84 Vadekar, R. D. (ed.), *Milinda Panho*, (Devanagari), Bombay, 1940.

85. Venkat Ramanam; *Nāgārjuna's Philosophy*, Bharatiya Vidya Prakashan, Varansi, 1971.

REFERENCE WORKS

1. Couch, T. W. (ed.), *Collier's Encyclopaedia*, 32 vols. P. F, Collier and Sons Corporation, New York, 1957.

2. Edward, P. (ed.), *Encyclopaedia of Philosophy* 8 Vols. Collier Macmillan Ltd., London, 1967.

3. Hastings, J. (ed.), *Encyclopaedia of Religion and Ethics*, 12 vols. T & T Clark, Edinburgh, London, 1925.

4. Ketkar G. V., *Maharashtriya Jnānakosa*, 22 vols. Maharashtriya Jnānakośa Mandal Ltd., Pune, 1923.

5. Monier, W., *A Sanskrit-English Dictionary*, Oxford University Press, London, 1951.

6. Runes, D. D., *Dictionary of Philosophy*, Philosophical Library, New York, 1942.

Index